PRAISE FOR
SHEPHERDS OF THE MIND

People today are dying for a trustworthy guide who can tend to the deep needs of their souls—especially in places of mental and emotional suffering. In *Shepherds of the Mind*, Tomy is just such a guide. Here, he not only leads readers on a path to healing, but to becoming a hope filled presence in the lives of others who are suffering. And taking his cues from Jesus, Tomy faithfully points us to the Good Shepherd whose relentless purpose and passion is to make us whole.

Michael John Cusick
Author of *Surfing for God* and *Sacred Attachment*

As someone who has experienced mental health struggles and walked with loved ones who do, I know firsthand that it cannot be ignored. And yet, it's not easy to discern how to best shepherd those who are in seasons of depression, anxiety, trauma, or grief. In *Shepherds of the Mind*, Tomy offers solid biblical insights and practical ministry counsel for those navigating difficult mental health seasons—their own or with others under their care. This resource is one you want on your bookshelf.

Michele Cushatt
Author of *A Faith That Will Not Fail: 10 Practices to Build Up Your Faith When Your World Is Falling Apart*

For the majority of my adult life, I have battled some profoundly deep and dark seasons of depression. What's even more humbling is that I am a pastor. You know, the guy we assume has it all together. I could not imagine navigating those seasons without Jesus, the Good Shepherd. This book is so timely for a culture that is experiencing mental health struggles at unprecedented levels. I absolutely love this book because it is saturated with grace, wisdom, compassion and, most importantly, personal confession.

Chad Bruegman
Lead Pastor, River Pointe Church in Richmond, TX
Former Founding Pastor, Red Rocks Church in Denver, CO

Tomy is one of the most genuine people I know, and that sincerity shows up on every page. His writing is vulnerable, practical, and flowing from real life—not theory. This book feels like a safe place to pause, wonder about your own story, and reflect on the people who trust you for care. It's a gift for anyone supporting others in ministry.

Brooklyn Lindsey
Youth Pastor, Somos Church in Lakeland, FL
CCO, Stuff You Can Use

When we experience chronic and arduous difficulties, it is God's people who step in and support us through the long haul. Tomy does a great job of educating and empowering believers to care for others in the depths of their pain. He provides sound advice, theological grounding, and realistic hope on how to sustain others through difficult seasons.

Dr. Veronica Johnson
Licensed Psychologist and Owner, Envision Counseling Clinic

SHEPHERDS OF THE MIND

CARING LIKE CHRIST IN AN AGE OF SILENT SUFFERING

TOMY A. CUMMINS

Stay Day Publishing
960 S. Interstate 25
Castle Rock, CO 80104

ISBN 979-8-9944225-1-9 (softcover)
ISBN 979-8-9944225-0-2 (hardcover)
ISBN 979-8-9944225-2-6 (ebook)
ISBN 979-8-9944225-3-3 (audio)

Cover design: Terry Dugan
Cover photo credit: youandigraphics @ Adobe Stock
Interior design: Ben Wolf, Inc.
Editing: Cristina Wright
Author Photograph: David Parks

First printing: 2026

Printed in the United States of America

CONTENTS

FOREWORD

I've learned something over the years: most pain doesn't announce itself.

It sits quietly in pews.

It sings the songs.

It volunteers.

It leads small groups.

And sometimes, it preaches the sermon.

Tomy's willingness to name his own journey through depression and suicidal desperation in this book only sharpened that awareness for me. We've all come face-to-face with people struggling with mental health. The question is, did we notice? And if we noticed, did we lean in—or quietly avoid? Because once you start telling the truth about pain, it becomes impossible to unsee how often it goes unnoticed.

That's why Ezekiel 34:4, which forms the roadmap for this book, has always felt uncomfortably honest to me. Not because it condemns bad intentions, but because it exposes blind spots. Places where even well-meaning care can move too fast, speak too loudly, or confuse strength with control. "With force and harshness you have ruled them"—not out of cruelty, but often out of fear, fatigue, or simply not knowing what else to do when faced with pain.

Tomy and this book name another way.

I appreciate its refusal to separate spiritual care from emotional reality. It assumes that ordinary believers—not just pastors or professionals—will encounter depression, trauma, anxiety, and even suicidal despair. Not as hypotheticals, but as painful interruptions in the lives of people they love. And instead of offering platitudes or pressure, this book offers sacred presence.

I remember meeting a cancer survivor in Rochester, Minnesota, at the Mayo Clinic. She had become a hero to many. Why? Because she fought—and she won. And yet after the cancer, she told me her greatest battles began. "The battles in the mind," she said, "are much harder than the battles in the body." That truth has stayed with me. After such a visible victory, she wasn't sure how to struggle, or whether she was even allowed to.

That's a lie many of us believe: *Why would I still be struggling when there has been so much victory in my life?*

Tomy helps us see that even as ordinary Christians—parents, friends, coworkers, small-group leaders, and yes, even pastors—we are all called to shepherd others, because we are all called to model our lives after the Good Shepherd. These chapters read like a slow retraining of the heart.

They remind us that care isn't about having the right answer, but about creating the kind of space where truth can be spoken safely, and healing can begin for those struggling with their mental health.

Remember: we are fighters. We are survivors.

This book also names a fear many of us carry but rarely admit—the fear of making things worse. The fear of saying the wrong thing. The fear that our presence might somehow cause harm instead of healing. Tomy meets that fear with wisdom and grace, reminding us that avoidance is rarely rooted in apathy, but in uncertainty—and faithful care begins not with perfection, but with courage.

And the book reminds us of something else we often forget: shepherds, of all kinds, need tending too.

This work makes room for our limits. For exhaustion. For the quiet ways caring for others can harden us if we're not careful. It invites us to care for ourselves—not as indulgence, but as an act of faithfulness.

Ultimately, Tomy keeps pointing us back to Jesus—the Good Shepherd who never forced, never shamed, never rushed pain. Who noticed the one. Who stayed. Who showed us that redemption often begins simply by being willing to draw near.

I'm grateful for Tomy and his courage to be honest. I've seen firsthand what happens when people hold truth and vulnerability together. Cultures shift. People exhale. Hope finds its way back into the room—maybe even your home, or the quiet halls of your heart.

I hope this book does the same for you as it has for me in real time. May it slow you down. May it sharpen your wisdom. May it remind you that God is already present in the pain you're being trusted to witness.

And may you discover, again, that all of this done in love still changes lives.

And one more thing: take off the cape.
There are no superheroes here.
Only shepherds.

Eric Samuel Timm
Pastor, Artist, Advocate
www.ericsamueltimm.com

A NOTE TO THE READER

Some of the stories and themes in this book touch on sensitive topics, including anxiety, depression, trauma, and suicide. If you have walked through these struggles personally—or love someone who has—you may find certain sections emotionally challenging. Please honor your own pace. Take breaks when needed. Pause to breathe and pray. Invite someone you trust to walk with you through the material if it feels heavy.

My intention is never to burden you, but to help you recognize both the depth of pain that others around you may be experiencing and the truth that you are not alone. The hope threaded through every chapter is the same hope at the center of our faith: the Good Shepherd draws near to the brokenhearted, and he never turns away from those in pain.

This book is not a substitute for professional mental health care. While I draw from evidence-based training and real pastoral experience, there are moments when a licensed therapist, counselor, or doctor is the safest and most appropriate next step for you and those you shepherd. If this book surfaces unresolved wounds or strong emotions, I encourage you to seek help—doing so is a sign of strength, not weakness. If at any point you feel unsafe, check Appendix A for some helpful resources.

Finally, I want to acknowledge the courage it takes to read a book like this. To engage thoughtfully with your own story or the suffering of someone you love requires both vulnerability and hope. My prayer is that, as you read, you will sense God's gentleness, his nearness, and his invitation to become a healing presence in a hurting world by the power of his Spirit.

You are seen.
You are loved.
And you are not alone.

Tomy

INTRODUCTION

SHEEP WITHOUT A SHEPHERD

When he saw the crowds, he had compassion for them, because
they were harassed and helpless, like sheep without a shepherd.
Matthew 9:36, ESV

THE WEIGHTS WE CARRY

I used to hunt. Well, it would be more accurate to say I used to go on long hikes through the forest while carrying a rifle. The truth is that I could count on one hand the number of times I even considered pulling the trigger, which means my rifle only ever served to help me burn more calories by carrying its weight. Still, I cherished those moments in God's creation, finding silence and solitude in the quiet forest. They provided space and time to think, pray, process, and meditate on scripture. Hunting also created opportunities to connect with the other men in my family, for which I was grateful.

The last time I went on one of those hunts that was more of a hike was in November 2021. I woke up long before the sunrise, hiked deep into a pitch-black forest in single-digit temperatures, and climbed onto a large rock formation overlooking an open meadow. I settled in and began praying as I watched the sun rise over the mountains in front of me. In that moment, I felt free. Free from the noise of the city. Free from the expectations that come with being a father and pastor. Free from the distracting buzz in my pocket that intermittently interrupts my day. It was nothing but space, time, and Jesus, and I loved every second of it.

As I took in the solitude that enveloped me, I found myself praying to God, "Show me where I need to surrender more of myself to you. Show me the things that are keeping me from better reflecting you to the world around me." This was my own personalized version of King David's prayer in Psalm 139:

Search me, God, and know my heart; test me and know my anxious thoughts. See if there is any offensive way in me, and lead me in the way everlasting.
PSALM 139:23-24

I didn't recognize it at the time, but looking back, I see what a bold —dare I say *risky*—prayer that was. What happened next felt like it happened all of a sudden, but in reality, it was over the course of a couple of hours of praying and processing: memories from my childhood and early adolescence began to surface; memories that I hadn't thought about in decades. Things I had deeply repressed because they were decidedly traumatic and abusive. Things that happened at the hands of people outside of my house. Things that had much further-reaching implications for my life than I could even begin to imagine in those moments.

At first, it was surreal, like I was reliving someone else's story. The memories were so foreign to me that it took me a while to come to terms with the fact that they were mine. I found myself thinking, "No, these are *my* memories . . . these things actually happened to me . . . I was actually *abused*." That prayer in the forest led to the hardest year of my life. On that day in the mountains by myself, I went from sitting on a boulder to feeling like I was being crushed beneath the weight of one.

Maybe some of you have never had to process a significant

amount of trauma—maybe some of you have or are currently—but we've all had to carry heavy things. We've all had to walk through hard seasons. And I can tell you from first-hand experience that, in the midst of those hard seasons in life, one of the enemy's greatest tools is to make us feel isolated. He will try to make us feel like we are the only ones struggling while everyone else is doing just fine. He will try to make us feel like no one else would understand—that everyone else has their own burdens, and it would be selfish to trouble our loved ones with our burdens. He whispers lies that we are too broken to be loved, too far gone to be helped.

The enemy uses shame to drive us further into isolation and hiding by making us think we are dirty or damaged beyond saving, so we'd do better to hide. He convinces us to do our best to carry those burdens alone, all the while putting on the best fake smile we can muster because if people knew the *real* us, we'd be rejected, despised, and scorned, and the accompanying shame would be too much to live through.

That was the very first thought that came rushing into my head once I came to terms with my trauma on that boulder, "You can't tell anyone. No one would want anything to do with you if they knew. No one would believe you anyway. You most definitely couldn't be a pastor anymore. Your wife would leave you if she knew because you are too broken, and it would be too much for her to handle; YOU would be too much for her to handle."

The enemy's lies can be terribly convincing, rattling around in our heads. Especially in our most vulnerable moments, those lies take root in some immensely damaging ways. Carrying the burden of these lies only adds to the weight of life that we are already struggling to carry, so the grief, the pain, and the brokenness compound, leaving us feeling crushed under their weight.

For me, on that boulder in the middle of the forest, the weight quickly felt like too much, and it led to despair. I couldn't see through the fog to a positive version of what life could be moving forward. The enemy knew this and offered me a solution, just as he did to Jesus standing on top of the temple in Jerusalem: "Throw yourself down."

The difference? He wanted Jesus to prove he wasn't alone. He wanted me to believe I was.

I am deeply grateful that this moment of suicidal desperation came *after* I had begun educating myself on mental health and suicide intervention techniques. The Holy Spirit brought to mind some of the very words I had spoken to others when they were in places of suicidal desperation. Words of presence, comfort, and hope (more on that later).

My journey toward healing began in earnest two days later when I arrived home from the hunting trip and quickly told my wife everything that had transpired. I invited her into the pain, and she lovingly and graciously joined me in that pain. I rejected isolation in favor of being known in a deeply intertwined community of mutually loving and sacrificial relationships, and I'm convinced it saved my life.

While I never would have asked to process this kind of trauma, I also wouldn't trade it for a multitude of reasons—some of which we will unpack later. One of the things I'm grateful for is how it helped me understand, on a new level, the depth of Jesus' compassion described in Matthew 9:

> When he saw the crowds, he had compassion for them, because they were harassed and helpless, like sheep without a shepherd.
> MATTHEW 9:36, ESV

CALLING ALL SHEPHERDS

My mental health journey that began on a boulder is far from unique in this era of mental health crises. Mental health struggles are rampant across a wide range of demographics, and the accompanying statistics show no signs of slowing.

My trek into the world of mental health education began (four years prior to the boulder experience) as I was working as a student pastor in Colorado Springs, Colorado. As a community, we collectively drew a stunned breath as ten students died by suicide in our area in the span of two weeks. I felt overwhelmed and ill-equipped to even know how to respond, much less to make a concerted effort to stem the tide of suicide contagion in our community. Along with several of my peers, I began to seek education on the topics of mental health and suicide. I became certified in programs designed to recognize signs of a potentially impending mental health crisis—programs that equipped us with tools on how to help those who are in the darkest places. I became certified in programs that aimed to intervene and even prevent suicide. I eventually became a trainer for several of these programs.

The more I educated myself on these sensitive topics, the more comfortable I became in holding space with those who are in places of deep pain. This is logical, of course. No matter how much we may *want* to build a house, it's impossible to build that house without being given the right tools and then being trained how to use those tools. That is the aim of our time together throughout this book: to give you a few tools from scripture so you may feel more and more qualified to step into the darkness and be the hands and feet of Jesus to the lost, hurting, and broken. Without the tools and the knowledge, it can be easy to edge away from a situation, saying, "I'm not qualified for this." And yet, we will certainly learn together that it's far less about being *qualified* and far more about being *present*.

It is indeed hard to be present for others on their mental health journey without feeling equipped to do so. I've seen this. Just a few years ago, I was sitting with a group of student pastors who very quickly became uncomfortable with the idea of preaching on the topic of mental health. One of them even claimed that his students—many of whom he affirmed were struggling with mental health—had directly told him, "We want to hear sermons about mental health, but not from you." The implication being that they wanted to hear from someone more qualified to speak on the subject than their student pastor. If that's true, kudos to those students for wanting to hear from a credible authority on the subject. In my experience, however, drowning people are too busy grasping at straws, hoping it will keep them afloat, to ask about the qualifications of anyone willing to jump into the water with them.

I can't really blame those student pastors. I've been where they were in that moment. In the immediate aftermath of the cluster of ten deaths by suicide that we watched unfold in those two weeks, we also had a student in *our* ministry survive a suicide attempt. Up until that point, none of the students who had died by suicide were directly involved in our student ministry (though we had several students deeply impacted by losing friends or classmates). When we got word that one of the students within our community had survived an experience of suicidal self-directed violence, I was absolutely frozen with fear and overwhelm. In the subsequent weeks, as that student reengaged at our student ministry, everything within me wanted to lean in and shepherd him as he worked toward health and healing, but some combination of fear, overwhelm, and feeling at an absolute loss for words kept me from leaning in fully. I would *try* to engage him. I would *try* to come alongside. More often than not, though, our conversations stayed shallow because of my own deep-seated sense of discomfort and fear of making it worse. This is exactly what it looks like to feel ill-equipped for many of us: avoidance. So, again, I can't really blame those student pastors.

Now, I certainly don't want to diminish the fact that significant damage has been done from pulpits all across America as pastors who are ill-equipped have spoken with authority on topics like mental health and suicide. I've watched as pastors have punitively and patronizingly categorized the mental health struggles of others with tired tropes that essentially tell them to have more faith or pray more, and they'll be healed. To be clear: prayer and faith are crucial to healing during and after a mental health crisis, but to say they are *all* that is needed is to significantly oversimplify a wildly complex issue. Mental health struggles are rarely one-dimensional. Almost all mental health struggles involve an interplay of social, emotional, physical, and spiritual factors—each influencing the others in ways that can't be separated or addressed in isolation. We are mind, body, and spirit. This isn't merely a belief held by secular psychology; scripture holds these delineations as well. In 1 Thessalonians 5:23, we read, "Now may the God of peace himself sanctify you completely, and may your whole **spirit and soul and body** be kept blameless at the coming of our Lord Jesus Christ" (ESV, emphasis added.) The Greek word for soul is *psuche*, which is where we get the word *psychology*. We are whole persons, so our mental health touches every part of who we are—our relationships, emotions, bodies, and spirits. Healing, therefore, requires care for the whole person.

I believe pastors who have taken this kind of "more faith, more prayer" stance to mental health are valiantly attempting to ensure that we don't turn to the things of this world for healing *in place of* turning to Jesus. I would wholeheartedly agree that Jesus needs to remain front and center in our focus. In fact, equipping us to show up to shepherd others as the hands and feet of Jesus will be the focus of this entire book. I disagree, however, with the false binary this line of thinking presents that seeking other forms of help—from a counselor, therapist, or other mental health provider—always means we are turning away from Jesus. Few people would say to someone in the middle of a crisis of a broken leg, "Pray more and have more faith, and you'll be healed." Why then would we say it for a mental health crisis? In cases of both mental health and physical health crises, it ought to be a both/and rather than an either/or. I vividly remember my sister Cristina fervently praying out loud over my niece as we sopped blood from her mouth after she smashed her face on a concrete parking block. It wasn't an either/or in that instance, but a both/and as we rushed her to the hospital. We should be ready and willing to point people toward Jesus *and* other faith-based mental health resources, knowing Jesus can use those resources to help them experience healing. If this feels like a foreign or uneasy topic, stick with me; we'll unpack it in greater detail later.

I certainly don't mean to share those stories as an indictment of my fellow clergy members—it would also be an indictment of myself if so—but only to illustrate that the tools needed to walk with someone through a mental health crisis are learned skills. Without them, even vocational ministers can be tempted to make excuses rather than hold space with those who are deeply hurting. As I've shared, the truth is, before my own educational experiences on the subject, I was the student pastor making excuses and choosing avoidance over presence.

What is clear to me is that avoidance leaves a void (duh) in relational, spiritual shepherding in an age that needs it more than ever. I'm convinced the church doesn't need more experts; it needs more present, patient, Spirit-led shepherds. And stick with me when I talk about shepherd lay-leaders; I'm not merely talking about more vocational ministers. I'm specifically talking about *you*. As followers of Jesus, we are all called to spiritually shepherd others because we are all called to make disciples. In fact, it was the last thing Jesus said in Matthew's gospel, and I'm convinced that, if he had been holding a microphone as he addressed the crowd, he would have dropped it right before he ascended into heaven.

> Jesus came and told his disciples, "I have been given all authority in heaven and on earth. Therefore, go and make disciples of all the nations, baptizing them in the name of the Father and the Son and the Holy Spirit. Teach these new disciples to obey all the commands I have given you. And be sure of this: I am with you always, even to the end of the age."
> MATTHEW 28:18-20, NLT

Again, this commissioning wasn't intended just for the vocational ministers among us, but for all of us who claim to be followers of Jesus. It's not just what we are called to *do*; it's who we are called to *be*. At my current church, we say we are "Changed lives, changing lives." We are all called to be disciples of Jesus who make disciples of Jesus— to learn his way of life, to live his commands, and to reflect his heart. This is what church leaders for centuries have called *spiritual formation*. The one clear command that Jesus gave to his followers:

> A new command I give you: Love one another. As I have loved you, so you must love one another. By this everyone will know that you are my disciples, if you love one another.
> JOHN 13:34-35

He didn't just say to love. He didn't even say to love well. He said to love the way he loved. And how did he love? If you asked Matthew, he'd point out how Jesus' love freed him from the shame of being a tax collector. If you asked Peter, he'd say how Jesus' love spoke life into him and still believed in him even at his lowest moment. If you asked the lepers, they'd tell you how Jesus' love touched them when they were untouchable.

Learning to make disciples and love like Jesus is the ultimate goal of spiritual formation. As Pastor John Mark Comer so eloquently but so simply puts it, our call is to "Be with Jesus. Become like Him. Do as He did."[1] And if we are going to become like him and do as he did, we are going to become shepherds. After all, Jesus is the Good Shepherd.

EXPECTATIONS FOR SHEPHERDS

So, if we are all supposed to be spiritual shepherds, cool, but what does that even mean? Shepherding metaphors are plentiful in the Bible. From King David's iconic and pastoral Psalm 23 to Jesus donning the title of Good Shepherd in John 10, and lots of stops in between. Shepherding language is abundant throughout scripture, which means books unpacking the concepts of spiritual shepherding are abundant as well, so we won't spend a ton of time unpacking all of the subtlety and nuance that comes with the shepherding metaphor.

For our purposes together, I'm more interested in getting straight to the brass tacks of what the expectations are that come with the role of spiritual shepherd. Luckily for us (but not so luckily for the spiritual shepherds of Israel), there is a singular verse in scripture that serves as a great list of expectations. It wasn't so lucky for them because the verse in question actually points out all of the ways they were getting it wrong.

The weak you have not strengthened, the sick you have not healed, the injured you have not bound up, the strayed you have not brought back, the lost you have not sought, and with force and harshness you have ruled them.
Ezekiel 34:4, ESV

It stands to reason that if the spiritual shepherds of Israel were getting chastised for not meeting these expectations, then inverting this list becomes a great framework for how to spiritually shepherd others well—maybe even especially those sheep experiencing a mental health crisis. And here's the good news: these are all achievable, especially considering that we are carriers of the Holy Spirit, which means we are carriers of healing, hope, and the powerful presence of Jesus. And as carriers of the Holy Spirit, holding space with hurting people is far more about availability than it is about ability. After all, the Holy Spirit will do the heavy lifting and is the only one capable of bringing healing. In his grace, God *chooses* to use us in spite of our own brokenness to help shepherd others as they walk toward healing and wholeness. My friend Bob calls this a *divine collaboration.*

Rest assured that by reading this book, you are not signing on to become a mental health care provider or to carry anyone else's crushing weight *for* them lest you, too, be crushed. You're not even signing on to try to fix them. We'll leave the counseling to the counselors, the therapy to the therapists, and the healing to the Holy Spirit. My hope and prayer are that, by inviting you into the story of my own mental health journey and sharing some of the tools I've been given, you will feel equipped by the Holy Spirit to step in, lean in, and help others know they aren't alone on their mental health journeys. I want to equip you to participate in that divine collaboration as you help the lost, hurting, and broken in your life to know that depression, anxiety, panic attacks, loneliness, shame, trauma, burnout, heartbreak, hopelessness, fear, perfectionism, insecurity, grief, and thoughts of suicide don't have to have the last word in their lives.

In the pages that follow, we will walk step by step through the picture God gives in Ezekiel 34:4—not as a legalistic list to check off, but as a call to live with gentleness, presence, and purpose. And since Ezekiel 34:4 is an indictment and not a blueprint, we will seek to live out a redemptive reversal of the failure of those spiritual shepherds in Israel. So, we will work backward. We begin in the first chapter by reversing the indictment of ruling with force and harshness by answering the call to lead gently. The subsequent chapters will then break down seeking the lost by learning to recognize cries for help, rounding up the strays by showing love to those who are trying to keep us at arm's length, binding up the injured by being present in moments of crisis, healing the sick by helping them anchor their identity in Christ and speaking truth into and over their lives, and then strengthening the weak by helping them build resilience for the long road ahead. After all, healing doesn't begin with commands; it begins with presence. So, before we learn to strengthen someone else's faith, we must learn to sit with them in their pain.

WOUNDED HEALERS

I already shared that my healing journey started the moment I chose to share what I was walking through with my wife Mendy. I told her about the trauma and the thoughts of suicide, even with the enemy shouting in my ear that sharing with her would end my life as I knew it. He was right, of course, but not in the way he was trying to convince me. The grace, love, and support that my beautiful wife showered on me every step of the journey served to strengthen our relationship in the end. There were plenty of hard days in between, but her response gave me confidence to invite others into my healing journey as well.

Over the course of the next several weeks and months, we created concentric circles around us of trust and support. It's hard enough to walk a path of pain toward healing, but imagine having to do it publicly as a pastor. I felt called by God early on to lead through that season with great vulnerability and honesty. I'm incredibly grateful for the leadership of my church that allowed me to preach sermons in our adult services that were raw and authentic. Those raw sermons helped create psychological and emotional safety for others to talk about the paths they were walking as well.

The further out those concentric circles went, the more careful I was with what and how I shared. Only Mendy and my therapists knew the intimate details of my trauma. The congregation hearing my testimony through sermons knew far less than my closest coworkers, who knew far less than my dearest friends and family. There were times I began sharing only to realize that some were not ready to hear my story or sit with me in my pain. There were also people who so clearly and empathetically communicated what an honor it was to help carry this burden with me as I walked the path of healing that God was laying out before me. And, friends, the healing that God brought to me was more than I could have ever imagined. I don't know what else to say other than to quote my Grandma Bennie, who often said, even in the midst of her own pain and suffering, "The good Lord has just been so good to me."

In a way that I could have never understood before this season, I now understand what it means that it is an honor to carry someone else's pain—not *for* them, but *with* them. Before my trauma journey, even as a pastor, I often found myself essentially patting people on the head from a distance like a sweet, southern grandma saying, "You poor thing," rather than leaning in and drawing close like a true shepherd.

You may not feel like a shepherd. You may not feel strong, equipped, or wise. That's okay. What matters is that you're willing to walk with someone, even when the path forward is unclear. You don't have to have all the answers, and you certainly don't have to be perfect. You just have to be willing to be used by God.

Priest, psychologist, and author Henri Nouwen popularized the term *wounded healer*. I love that! We are all wounded by the sin, brokenness, and corruption of this world. Rarely do we choose to experience those wounds, though we occasionally might make choices that cause the wounds to happen. Our choice is whether or not we walk the path toward healing. And then we get to choose to make ourselves available to be used by God to be part of the healing journey for others. Being wounded is inevitable. Becoming a wounded healer is a choice. The world is full of silent suffering, but the Good Shepherd is still speaking, and he is inviting us to follow him—not just for our sake, but for the sake of others as well.

In Isaiah 2:2-5, the prophet Isaiah paints a beautiful picture of an age to come when everyone will hunger and thirst to follow after God's ways. He says weapons will be beaten into harvesting tools, and no one will learn the art of war any longer. When we look at the world around us, it might feel like that vision is still a long way off, but verse 5 serves as an invitation to not just look forward, but to step into this way of living *now*.

> O house of Jacob, come, let us walk in the light of the LORD.
> ISAIAH 2:5, ESV

In Isaiah's mind, living this way now isn't naive idealism; it is prophetic realism. We live in a broken world, and though we must live in the world as it *is*, we act in line with the world as it *will be*. One day, the eastern sky will tear open, and God will arrive to take his place as King. Until that day comes, Paul exhorts us to live as citizens of heaven in the here and now.[2] That's what Jesus did, and it's what the church is called to do.

So, come friends, let us walk in the light of the Lord as wounded healers. Let us shepherd the hurting, the lost, and the broken by the healing power of God's Holy Spirit at work in us and through us. Let us make ourselves available to be used by God to help his kingdom come until it is on earth as it is in heaven.

SELF-CARE AND REFLECTION

In each chapter, we will end with an encouragement to take care of yourself well (often referred to as self-care) and to spend a few minutes in reflection. Reading about topics like abuse, self-harm, and suicide is a weighty endeavor. Surrendering that weight to Jesus is crucial. If we don't take time to decompress, we will carry that weight with us the rest of the day and impact others around us. The truth is that God may want to burden you in specific ways as you read this book. In fact, that's my hope and prayer: as we read, may he break our hearts for what breaks his heart to the point that it stirs us to action. So, know that self-care is not intended to be an activity aimed at intentionally ignoring God's Spirit speaking to us. It is not a turning *away*, but a turning *toward*. It is a recentering of ourselves onto the goodness, mercy, and presence of God in the midst of our burden for others. Don't rush past this crucial recentering process.

If you're not sure how to practically engage in self-care, feel free to skip ahead to chapter nine (specifically, the Choose Your Own Adventure segment at the end) before you move on to chapter one, so you can use the tools in that chapter as you go through this book. I would also encourage you to journal a few thoughts on what you feel God is speaking to you at the end of each chapter. Pay attention to what words and concepts stand out, what you feel, and where you feel burdened. For some of you, the provided space will feel wildly inadequate. If that's you, I'm guessing you already have several journals to choose from, so have at it. In fact, maybe self-care might look like buying a shiny new leather-bound journal just for our journey together– you're welcome! For some, the idea of filling the provided space will feel daunting. Just write a few words that capture your thoughts and feelings. Author James Clear tells us that we can't improve on a habit that we don't already have, so start small and build from there. My hope and prayer are that by the time you get to the end of the book, you will be able to look back on what you've written and pick up on an emerging theme. Pay attention to that theme. God is speaking to you through it.

Today, I will care for myself and stay connected to God by:

Space for Reflection:

xxix

ONE
LEAD GENTLY

Come to me, all who labor and are heavy laden, and I will give you rest.
Take my yoke upon you, and learn from me, for I am gentle and
lowly in heart, and you will find rest for your souls.
For my yoke is easy, and my burden is light.
MATTHEW 11:28-30, ESV

THE DARKEST VALLEY

Roughly an hour of my life is missing. There are brief snapshots like Polaroids[1] of memory sprinkled throughout, but the full timeline had to be reconstructed later. There is a Polaroid of me in the ambulance. Another of someone sending me to a different hospital that had a better neurology unit. A flurry of activity from the many doctors and nurses around me in the emergency room, and the inane thought that I should find a way to humorously tell them what a good job they were doing to help cut the tension. The hum of the CT machine checking for brain bleeds. My wife wincing at the sight of the neck brace. Sadly, the first *vivid* memory I have that isn't shrouded with a thick, hazy fog is having my road rash scrubbed to remove gravel and other debris. I really wish I had still been too out of it to feel every excruciating moment.

About an hour or so before the torturous scrubbing of my road rash, I crested the top of a steep hill about fifteen miles into a twenty-mile bike ride with my sister Cristina. We had both recently gotten into road cycling. Cresting the top of that hill was the last thing I remembered of the ride before our steep descent down the other side. My sister later recounted the traumatic experience of watching me veer out of the bike lane to avoid an object, only to encounter another hazard that sent me straight down to my side at about thirty miles per hour. In the lingo of the extreme sports world, they would say I immediately "rag-dolled," which means I was knocked unconscious and my body went completely limp. I slid another thirty or so feet on my side before my head hit a curb, which flung me spinning around nearly 360 degrees like a top.

My sister was certain she had just watched me die. After she told the paramedics what she had witnessed, they wasted no time getting me to the hospital and into triage; the signs were pointing to a brain bleed. (Spoiler alert: I'm still alive thanks to my Bell cycling helmet, but I did, indeed, fracture my skull in four different places around the orbital socket of my right eye.) The next year or so was the darkest of my life up until that point (the boulder moment wouldn't come for another five years). I suffered a traumatic brain injury (TBI) that led to months of side effects—the most prominent of which was *aphasia*. Aphasia makes it difficult to find words. I would know that I wanted my wife to pass me the eating thing with pointy spears on the end, but the word *fork* would evade me.

I'm sure you can imagine how hard it would be to not be able to find words for someone whose identity was, in many ways, wrapped up in preaching. The aphasia, coupled with a negative reaction to pain medication, led to a long season of depression. It wasn't the first time I had gone through a season of depression, and it wouldn't be my last. Somehow, it wasn't until I began my trauma therapy years later (after the boulder) that I recognized the pattern of depression in my life that dated back to college. The depression stemming from my TBI was a dark one, but it is futile to compare pain.

At its worst, each season of depression made it hard to get out of bed or find the energy or desire to do . . . well, anything. My self-image and self-worth were shot. My internal dialogue was dark. Seasons of depression nearly cost me at least one job, but in that particular instance, I quit before they could escalate to the point of firing me. I've never seen a more relieved look on the face of an employer. I was too numb to be offended.

THE RIGHT TO BE HEARD

Looking back on each of those different seasons of depression, I can now see ways in which people showed up well for me. Their actions and presence created emotional safety that built relational trust. Others tried to help in ways that hurt. Some saw glimpses of the downward spiral I was on and tried to warn me what was at the bottom in humorous ways before, essentially, telling me to suck it up. Coworkers made snide comments out of frustration or resentment that I wasn't carrying my fair share of the load; their frustration was completely warranted.

The people who made a positive impact during each spell of depression all had a similar characteristic in their approach: they were gentle. They approached me with care, humility, and grace. They tended to ask questions more often than they made blanket statements. They were willing to be present and continue to show up even when I wasn't at my best. In the mental health world, this is often referred to as *holding space.* In short, those friends and loved ones earned the right to be heard by showing up as the hands, feet, and mouthpiece of Jesus, speaking love and compassion into my life. It would be hard to think of someone who showed up for me in those ways during each season of depression who isn't still a dear friend to this day.

I've been on both sides of mental health struggles enough to know how hard it can be to watch someone—especially a loved one—walk through seasons of pain, struggle, doubt, depression, or even suicidal desperation. It's hard to play the long game in those scenarios. We want so badly to help that we tend to come on too strong, offering solutions before we've even taken the time to listen. Like running at a trapped and wounded animal instead of approaching with slow, cautious movements, our aggressive or forceful actions only serve to cause them to put their defenses up even more.

We probably don't even recognize what we are doing, but often, trying to rush someone through a season like this has more to do with helping ourselves than it does with helping them. Again, we don't mean to, but essentially, we are communicating to them, "I need *you* to feel better so *I* can feel better because this situation is too much for me." Trying to help with quick, pat answers or solutions is the opposite of holding space for them. I don't know about you, but rarely am I willing to follow unsolicited advice that oversimplifies a complex issue, because rarely is it helpful. It's not gentle. It's not like Jesus.

A ME-SHAPED LENS

I'm an Enneagram 9. I know that even reading the word *Enneagram* might make some of you put your guard up. I completely understand. I've seen the Enneagram wielded as a weapon, used to oversimplify and dehumanize others by putting them in a box. I've also witnessed it exalted and revered so highly that it is regarded as an authority on par with scripture. These uses of the Enneagram are wrong, harmful, and unbiblical. At its worst, the Enneagram can indeed become an object of fixation or outright worship, which is idolatry. At its best, however, the Enneagram is simply a personality assessment tool aimed at fostering self-awareness by helping identify common traits and tendencies for each of the nine personality types.[2]

I have found the Enneagram to be a wildly helpful spiritual development and relational awareness tool, and this is how we will talk about the Enneagram in this book: it's a tool, no more. Author, former pastor, and Enneagram expert Ian Morgan Cron was told by a Benedictine monk and spiritual director, "For centuries, great Christian teachers have said knowing yourself is just as important as knowing God. Some people will say that's feel-good psychology when actually it's just good theology."[3] This statement to Cron echoes theologian John Calvin's insistence that "Without knowledge of self, there is no knowledge of God."[4] I've found that to be simultaneously painfully and encouragingly true. Self-awareness helps us better identify the movement of the Holy Spirit as he shapes us to look more like Jesus. This process is easier to engage in when we work to know ourselves better. As a type 9, I am what is known as a "peacemaker." Please stem your tide of jealousy at the fact that we nines are the only type counted as *blessed* by Jesus. Type 8, calm down; it's just a joke! And type 4, don't worry, you're special, too, just like everyone else. (If you don't get those jokes, don't worry, it's very niche and nerdy, so you're definitely not alone.) Knowing our Enneagram type can be helpful because it can help us recognize the lens through which we see Jesus.

We all have lenses through which we read scripture. These lenses shape what pops out to us as we read. We read scripture through cultural lenses, worldview lenses, historical lenses, etc. These lenses, like rose-colored glasses, color the way we see the world around us— or at least, that's what I'm told; I'm colorblind. Ultimately, all of these lenses form together to create a me-shaped lens based on our experiences, opinions, and wiring. My Enneagram 5 friends, who are known as the "investigators," come alive when they see Jesus at the Temple as a young boy, having rich theological discussions with the elders. My type eight friends, known as the "challengers," come alive when they see Jesus flipping tables and cleansing the temple.

It is not lost on me that as a type nine, I am more wired than most to be drawn to the patience with which Jesus led his disciples, the gentleness with which he met those who were hurting, and the kindness he extended to the ostracized. And while I acknowledge a proclivity to come alive at these moments more than others, I also would argue that there are far more stories that highlight Jesus' compassion than his righteous indignation. Either way, I hope we can at least agree that the instances of the righteous indignation of Jesus (my students would call it *saltiness*) are never pointed at those who are hurting or suffering. Jesus reserves his harshest words for the hard-hearted and his gentlest touch for the broken-hearted. As shepherds, this is the posture we should be seeking to adopt with our sheep, especially those who are hurting.

MET WITH GRACE AND COMPASSION

Like a spiritual triage, Ezekiel 34:4 follows the scope of neglect from less urgent to more urgent.

- Failing to strengthen the weak → ignored daily care
- Failing to heal the sick → ignored wounded or misplaced identity
- Failing to bind up the injured → ignored immediate pain
- Failing to round up the strays → ignored those who drifted away
- Failing to seek the lost → ignored those who were in the depths of despair
- Failing to lead with gentleness and compassion → ignored the humanity and inherent value of God's children

This progression reflects the descending spiral of neglect; as people grow weak, they become sick, then injured, then isolated, then lost entirely as those who are charged with their care fail to approach them with gentleness and compassion. A redemptive reversal of the indictment of Ezekiel 34:4 would start with leading and caring for our flock the same way that Jesus led and cared.

When the woman with the issue of blood in Luke 8 touched the hem of Jesus' garment after twelve years devoid of human contact because of the Jewish ritual cleansing laws, Jesus restored her humanity by calling her *daughter*. When a leper said, "If you are will-ing," Jesus was moved with compassion and healed him, saying, "I am willing."[5] When the religious elite presented a false binary of assuming a man was born blind because of his own sin or else the sin of his parents, Jesus rejected the notion that all suffering is the direct result of one's own sin.[6] With the sick and afflicted, there is no rebuke. No scolding. Just compassion and restoration.

The Samaritan woman at the well with a complicated past was met with dignity and offered living water, and she was transformed by the truth Jesus spoke.[7] The woman brought before Jesus to be stoned for adultery was defended and then forgiven by Jesus, as he then set her on a new trajectory.[8] Jesus honored Zacchaeus by going to his house —*before* Zacchaeus repented.[9] To the sinners and outcasts, Jesus spoke truth, but always in a way that lifted the lowly rather than crushing them.

Peter sank into the waves after taking his eyes off of Jesus, and Jesus said, "You of little faith, why did you doubt?"[10] A correction, yes, but offered as Jesus was catching Peter. The disciples were terrified when they first saw Jesus after the resurrection, but Jesus greeted them with peace, not judgment.[11] Thomas gained a new nickname by doubting the resurrected Jesus standing before him. Jesus invited Thomas to touch him and believe—not with anger, but with grace, because even when correcting doubt, Jesus did it in a relational, merciful way.

One brick at a time, one moment at a time, Jesus built a foundation of trust that created emotional safety for his disciples, for the sinners and outcasts, and for the sick and afflicted. And, to me, the greatest example of the depth of that emotional safety is on full display when Peter went fishing after Jesus was crucified. Fresh on Peter's mind and heart after the crucifixion was the shame of having denied Jesus three times. He felt so ashamed and lost that he went back to what he knew —his former life as a fisherman. And then he failed at that as well.

After a night of failing to catch a single fish, which I'm sure only served to compound Peter's feelings of shame and worthlessness, the disciples out on the boat encountered Jesus calling to them from land. When Peter recognized it was Jesus, he was so overcome by a desire to get to the very presence of Jesus that he couldn't wait for the others to get the boat back to land, so he disrobed, jumped into the water, and swam to shore. That is emotional and psychological safety: running *to* Jesus even after denying him three times rather than running *away* in shame. The trust Peter felt brings tears to my eyes.

Friends, if we want to shepherd others well through their mental health crises or their lowest moments in life, it has to start with building this kind of emotional safety for those we care about. To love them in such a way that, at their darkest moments, they turn to us—confident they will find not shame and judgment, but grace and compassion leading to restoration.

THE GRACE/TRUTH PARADOX

As of the writing of this book, I've been working in student ministry for over twenty-one years. Just writing that makes me feel old. I would struggle to come up with even a ballpark figure for the number of times I've wanted to grab a student by the collar, give them a dramatic shake, and yell, "JUST STOP! IF YOU'LL JUST STOP DOING THE *STUPID* THING YOU'RE DOING, YOUR LIFE WOULD BE SO MUCH BETTER!" Don't worry, I've never once actually done it. It reminds me of the scene in the Jim Carey movie *Liar, Liar* where his legal advice to one of his clients is shouted into a phone held at arm's length, "STOP BREAKING THE LAW [DUMMY]!" Fair warning: don't search the clip because he doesn't say, "Dummy."

Who knows, maybe this kind of indignation against watching sin wreck someone's life is completely appropriate, but we never see Jesus respond in this way. Even when Jesus pointed out the checkered past of the woman at the well, he said it very matter-of-factly with no color commentary to drive home the point in a shaming way. I've never seen someone's life transformed by the healing power of shame, because that's not a thing. I have, however, seen plenty of instances over the years where that kind of approach delivered abrasively and with elevated emotions is wildly harmful and destroys relational trust. It's reductive, punitive, and shaming. Especially in the realm of mental health, be very careful not to imply that someone's clinical anxiety, depression, etc., is their own fault. They might be engaging in self-destructive behaviors that are compounding the issue, but we'll get to how to help them replace those behaviors with more helpful ones later.

Now, hear me when I say that I'm not suggesting we avoid speaking truth, but that we carefully measure in grace when we speak that truth. John 1 presents us with a paradox:

> The Word became flesh and made his dwelling among us. We have seen his glory, the glory of the one and only Son, who came from the Father, full of grace and truth.
> JOHN 1:14

It doesn't say Jesus had some of each, but that he was full of both grace and truth. To be full of grace and truth simultaneously feels paradoxical. We can imagine one without the other because we've seen it. My friend and mentor Bob likes to say, "Truth without grace is violence." It is judgmental, bullying, and shaming. In a word, it's pharisaical. Inversely, I would say all grace with no truth is, to put it plainly, a bad friend. It is apathetic, careless, and avoidant. If I'm watching you blindly walk toward the edge of a cliff that you don't realize is there, but I choose not to say something because I'm afraid of hurting your feelings or infringing on your right to walk off that cliff . . . well, that's not very loving.

The goal, as we are transformed more and more into the likeness of Jesus, is to learn to bring both grace and truth to any given situation. Going back to the woman caught in adultery, Jesus met her with grace, saying, "Neither do I condemn you,"[12] but then he also set her on a new trajectory by speaking truth, saying plainly, "Go and sin no more."[13] This is both grace in truth in one breath: neither do I condemn you, but also, go and leave your life of sin. It meets her where she is, but refuses to leave her where she is. Not an either/or, but a both/and.

Finding the right balance in the tension between these two for any given situation is a Spirit-led art form. Tension isn't a bad thing, after all. It is the tension on a piano string that allows a note to ring out when a key is pressed. Find the right amount of tension, and it's beautiful when a skilled master musician sits at the keyboard and plays that piano. Too much or too little tension, and the sound is dissonant and unattractive. We need both grace and truth to find the beauty within the tension; then, we need to surrender our lives to the Master, so the song of our lives is compelling to the people around us. The question for us as shepherds is this: How do we bring both in a way that allows us to build emotional safety for those we love?

THE SUPPORT/CHALLENGE MATRIX

At my current church, we utilize a tool called the Support-Challenge Matrix.[14] In short, the concept of the matrix is all about learning to calibrate both support and challenge to liberate those we lead. Similar to being all truth and no grace, they would say that bringing all challenge and no support is domineering. It might get quick results, but this kind of leadership tanks the long-term sustainability of a team. People don't stay on those kinds of teams in the long term, and if someone has a healthy view of themselves, they will check out of relationships where they don't feel supported.

Inversely, bringing all support and no challenge is enabling. People might feel cared for, but they rarely move toward growth or health. Self-aware people know they aren't perfect, so failing to bring challenge will actually erode trust as they begin to think you are withholding truth from them. Both support and challenge are needed, but not always in equal measure, and not all the time. You have to put the relational change in your pocket before you can spend it in key moments of challenge, or else people end up feeling like you are not *for* them. Certainly, Jesus challenged Peter; at one point, Jesus told Peter, "Get behind me Satan," when Peter unknowingly tried to get Jesus off mission. But this high challenge came on the heels of Jesus speaking significant truth into Peter's life. In fact, this moment came immediately after Jesus changed his name from Simon to Peter, which means "rock." And trust me when I say, Jesus gave Peter this new name "Rock" long before Peter was stable and mature.

I have to imagine that Peter only psychologically recovered from being called Satan because he had also been called the Rock. He recovered because he had already experienced so many moments of tender compassion and loving acceptance from Jesus. Peter *became* the rock *because* Jesus liberated him with both grace and truth, support and challenge, until he lived out of his fullest potential through the power of the Holy Spirit. I mentioned earlier that we have to earn the right to be heard. So, how do we earn that right to be heard—besides bringing both support and challenge? Let's continue to take our cues from Jesus.

WITNESS THROUGH WITH-NESS

The first way we can build trust and safety as we seek to lead gently is simply by showing up. Relationships, ultimately, are built through shared experiences, which means our witness is built through *with-ness,* as my friend Bobby likes to say. The more time we spend with people, the more opportunities there are to build trust. Young Life, a student-focused parachurch ministry, touts the importance of "creatively wasting time" with students in order to create opportunities for discipleship. This means every moment of laughter, every moment of silliness, and every moment of shared joy is ultimately an investment in building relational equity. And as we've already discussed, you have to put change in your pocket before you can spend it.

Showing up for fun will buy opportunities to show up in pain. Showing up in pain will, in an accelerated way, buy opportunities to speak truth into the lives of those we love. All the stories we read in the New Testament about Jesus doing ministry with and in the presence of his disciples account for just a fraction of the three years or so they spent together. They were together constantly in those three years, and like good apprentices, those disciples were soaking up everything they could from Jesus. We don't know exactly how all of that time was spent, but we can surmise one thing: Jesus was building relational equity with his disciples. All of the big moments we read about in scripture were being supplemented with tons of smaller, in-between moments—and yet *smaller* and *in-between* do not mean lacking in significance. Jesus was building trust. He was creating emotional safety so that when Peter was at the bottom of a deep, dark spiral of shame, the moment he laid eyes on Jesus after the resurrection, Peter was compelled to run *to* Jesus rather than *away*.

Being a support for someone on their mental health journey doesn't mean exclusively sitting in the pain with them. At times, and following their cues, it means helping them remember that there is joy, laughter, and fun to be experienced. I have friends who are walking parties waiting to happen. If that sounds like you, this is where you will shine as your joyous presence will help the hurting see that it's okay to laugh and experience joy.

There will also be a need to sit in the pain—to show up for people when they are at their lowest. We will spend far more time unpacking how to show up for others in their pain in chapter four. Some dear friends, the Bluebaughs, did this for me on my trauma journey and helped coin the phrase "Sitting in the suck." A lot of what we'll discuss on suck-sitting, I learned from them. They were also great at reading the right moments and injecting some fun on that journey when we were up for it. Those moments reminded me it's okay to laugh now and then, even in the darkest valleys. In either instance, sitting in the suck or laughing in the valley, they were Jesus to us just by being present. They didn't bail when things got hard. They leaned in, and their with-ness was their witness. Thanks, Tay and Ste. Let's keep leapfrogging!

INVITE, DON'T PRESSURE

How's it going? How are you? How are things? These questions are simple enough, and some of the more common greetings in America. I'm actually a big fan of these questions, except that I hate them as a casual greeting, and here's why: too often, they are insincere. Way too often, we ask such questions hoping or expecting that the other person will say, "Good," and keep moving right along. I've certainly made the mistake of asking these questions only to have someone take it as an actual invitation to open up. Next thing I know, they are three minutes into sharing about the hardship of their last week, and I realize I have to be on the platform to preach in less than five minutes.

My friend David encouraged me to start saying, "It's good to see you," instead of asking, "How are you doing?" Asking the question when we don't really have time to hear the answer adds to a sense of isolation for those who are hurting. It reinforces the lie that no one really cares or really wants to hear the hard things they have to say. So now, I assure you, if I ask the question, it's an actual invitation to open up; if you'd like to, of course.

There is a delicate balance between making a sincere invitation for someone to share about their struggles and becoming nosy. I've experienced perfectly executed invitations from loving, caring individuals who made me feel safe and seen in my pain, but I didn't always take them up on the invitation to share. I still felt validated that they asked, but the truth was, I already had my support system, or else I wasn't ready to share. It is helpful to remind ourselves that we might not be one of their people, and that's okay as long as they have someone.

I've also experienced both ends of the spectrum that exist on either side of that loving invitation. I've experienced what it's like to have people clam up and shut down the second I start sharing about my experience with trauma. Thankfully, these moments came after I had moved toward healing and wholeness, or else they might have done significant damage. It might have led to thoughts like, "Why try again? I already gave it a shot, and people weren't willing to help. Maybe I really *am* too much." In Romans 12:9, Paul exhorted us to, "Let love be genuine" (ESV). Be careful not to extend an invitation if you're not ready or able to sit and listen as someone opens up about their experiences. For your sake, but also for theirs. Such an empty invitation could serve to reinforce negative self-talk that they are *too much* or that *no one cares.* Often, the unspoken expectation that hurting people feel is, "Please act like you're okay, even if you're not . . . for my sake." It leads to further self-isolation.

At the other end of the spectrum, I've had the misfortune of having people ask inappropriately invasive and nosy questions simply to satisfy their desire to be *in the know*. The truth is, we don't get to demand to be part of someone's support system. We don't get to choose which concentric circle we occupy. Paul also reminded us that love doesn't demand its own way.[15] If you just *have* to know, you likely aren't inquiring out of love, but maybe out of morbid curiosity. In Matthew 11, when Jesus said, "Come to me," it wasn't a command; it was an invitation. Opening up and accepting the invitation is our job. Work on finding the beauty between making a sincere invitation to carry someone's burdens with them without crossing the line into being pushy or nosey, and you will find yourself gaining significant trust with those around you.

LISTEN WITH OPEN HANDS AND AN OPEN HEART

If you really want to learn to create emotional safety and build trust by leading gently, here's where the money is: hone your active listening skills. Being a good listener is becoming a lost art. I'm sure if you closed your eyes, took a deep breath, and pictured the best listener you know, two things will probably be true:

1. It probably won't take you very long to scroll through your mental contacts before you definitively know who owns the title of Best Listener in your life. That's likely true because of a mixture of how rare people like that are and also what a special place they likely hold in your heart. If you struggle to think of someone, I'm sorry. Unfortunately, people like this are becoming rare.
2. If you do have someone who occupies that spot, you will probably feel a bit better just thinking about them because I'm betting they are someone who makes you feel seen, known, and valued. They make you feel safe. Even thinking of a safe person who feels attuned, trustworthy, and emotionally available can cause the amygdala in your brain to reduce threat signaling, your prefrontal cortex to regain the ability to reason, and your attachment system to

activate, causing you to feel safer. In short, your brain has filed them away as a reference point of stability, and you will feel that stability just by thinking about them.

So, how can you be more like that person? What do they do that makes them such great listeners? What do they do that makes you feel seen, known, and safe? Essentially, what I'm asking is, how are they like Jesus to you? How are they gentle and humble—the way Jesus described himself?

I actually feel blessed to know several great listeners, but from a young age, the best model for me was always my mom Judy. *Nanny*, as she's affectionately known by all of her grandkids, is an Enneagram 2, the helper, so she's naturally wired to *want* to carry others' burdens with them. In my lifetime, I've seen her be a safe space for more people than I can count. I'm guessing there is a multitude of people who have lost touch with her for various reasons through the years, but I'm confident that if any of them ran into her at a coffee shop, they would feel immediately safe enough with her to share what's been going on in their lives since they were last together. "God, what a gift to be my mother's child."[16]

Great listeners, like my mom, listen with open hands and an open heart. Warmth and invitation are exuding from them because they aren't thinking about what to say next; they are genuinely listening. They are fully present. Any comment from a great listener is an encouragement to keep going or to clarify what was said. They give verbal and visual feedback through simple cues like nodding and making soft eye contact while saying things like, "Hmmm," with a tone of compassion rather than pity.

Great listeners make sure that their facial expressions and body language match the tone of the conversation. Often, they literally will open their hands on their laps as if they are receiving a gift from someone as they listen. They don't rush to fill the silence, but let it linger as an invitation into a sacred space together. They are quicker to respond to emotion and comment with words like, "That sounds really painful," knowing people need to be felt before they can be helped. They also normalize others' emotions by saying things like, "Of course you were overwhelmed by that; who wouldn't be?"

Great listeners are also quick to honor the difficulty of sharing by making sure people know they don't have to share more than they want to share. Again, they invite rather than pressure. They hold space while letting the other person take the lead.

Great listeners are slow to share any personal anecdotes or similar experiences unless they are invited to do so. They know that chiming in with their own stories will make the conversation about them and, possibly, even diminish what someone else is sharing. They reserve judgment, offer grace, and never share advice without being asked for it. Or at the very least, they ask for permission first, saying, "Would it be ok if I shared some of my experiences in this area?"

Finally, great listeners thank others for trusting and honoring them by sharing part of their story. As it's appropriate, they will offer an apology, not in an attempt to take ownership over what happened to the person sharing, but as a way of saying, "That should have never happened to you, and I'm sorry you had to carry that weight."

Let's pause for a moment. Our Cummins family motto is, "Never let a good thought go unsaid." I'd encourage you to take a minute or ten to either text or call the person you've just been picturing and thank them for being such a great listener. Be specific. And let love be genuine.

MAKING IT RIGHT

A few years ago, my wife started using the phrase with our kids, "We won't always get it right, but we will always make it right." She's a keeper, y'all. I've never met anyone quicker to own her mistakes than Mendy. I often hear her going to our children and saying things like, "I'm sorry. Mommy shouldn't have talked to you that way. Will you forgive me?" It's changed my own leadership style with my student ministry team by watching the way she parents our kiddos. I try to be just as quick to apologize and make it right when I miss the mark, which is more often than I'd like to admit.

Walking with people through any sort of hurt, habit, or hangup—to borrow language from Celebrate Recovery[17]—is going to be messy. They aren't perfect, and neither are we. Being part of someone's support system is truly an honor, but it's also hard, which means we won't always get it right. We will make mistakes. We will run out of patience at times. We will rush to fix. Few things will build emotional safety like owning up to our mistakes and repairing the relationship when we know we got it wrong. Some of the people I respect the most in this world are those who are quickest to own their mistakes.

In the Cummins Casa, we practice the five-part apology. There are several versions of this floating around,[18] but the Cummins version is slightly modified.

1. "I'm sorry for…"
   a. Be specific. It shows ownership for one's actions.
2. "I know it made you feel…" or "I know it hurt you because…"
   a. Acknowledge how your actions impacted the other party involved. It empathetically says, "I see you."
3. "Next time I will . . ."
   a. How will I avoid hurting you in that way again, or how will I try to do it better next time? It shows a desire and intention for growth.
4. "Will you forgive me?"
   a. We can't demand forgiveness; we can simply own what we did and ask for it. It leaves those we've hurt with a sense of agency.
5. "How can I make it better?"
   a. This is an offer for restitution. Often in our household, the answer is as simple as, "With a hug," to repair the connection. Sometimes, it's a request for space to process emotions. Once again, it gives the other person agency and a chance to advocate for what they need in the moment. If they ask for space, give it to them.

> Forgiveness can be done quickly; repairing the
> relationship will often take time and thoughtfulness.

Imagine walking with someone who has been deeply wounded and is walking through a tough season. Can you also imagine what it would feel like to them to be offered this kind of intentional and thoughtful apology? Making it right can do more than just repair your relationship with that person; it can help offer them healing.

DON'T FORGET YOUR SUPERPOWER

For a brief moment in kindergarten, I completely forgot that I was really good at throwing a Frisbee. I know it sounds ridiculous, but it's true.[19] It wasn't until just before my third and final throw at the frisbee toss station at field day that my mom caught my attention and told me, "Just throw it like you do at home." That simple statement reawakened something that I should have never forgotten. "Oh, yeah, I know how to throw a frisbee, like, *really* far!" No joke, I stepped up to the line, threw the frisbee further by far than anyone else that day, and took first place in the frisbee toss.

Let's not make the same mistake in our quest to walk alongside others in their pain as we lead gently. Don't forget your superpower: the Holy Spirit. Praying and leaning into the Spirit's promptings will set us up for success better than anything else. Through the years, I've learned that it's okay to take a deep breath and ask the Spirit for guidance when a moment feels too big for me. Those have actually been some of the most powerful moments of my life because I know what transpired next didn't happen out of my own strength, abilities, or wisdom.

Remember, we don't have to have all the answers; we just have to make ourselves available. Availability matters more than ability because it's ultimately God's job to heal them, not ours. Leading gently will feel less like a legalistic command to obey truth and more like a compassionate invitation to live out of an identity that is rooted in truth. Take time each day to work on surrendering more and more of yourself to the power and presence of God's Spirit in your life. Take a cue from seventeenth-century monk, Brother Lawrence, and practice the presence of God.[20] Whenever you're alone, talk to God as if he's right there, because guess what? He is! Learning to lean into the Spirit in low-risk moments will make it much easier to lean into God's Spirit when more is at stake.

Gentleness is not passivity; it is participation in the power of God's Spirit in our divine collaboration. To lead gently is to trust that love does more lasting work than force ever could. Every time we choose presence over pressure, compassion over control, and prayer over panic, we reflect the heart of the Good Shepherd—the one who leads us gently home. You were never meant to lead and shepherd by sheer effort, but by surrendered presence. The same Spirit that hovered over the waters of creation now hovers over your moments of presence with the lost and hurting, waiting to breathe life through your gentle leading.

SELF-CARE AND REFLECTION

Today, I will care for myself and stay connected to God by:

Space for Reflection:

TWO
SEEK THE LOST

For the Son of Man came to seek and save the lost.
Luke 19:10

THE UN-ASKABLE QUESTION

"**A**re you thinking about killing yourself?" Throughout my mental health and suicide intervention training, I learned the importance of asking this question directly. Don't leave room for interpretation. Don't beat around the bush. Just ask it. Vague questions rarely get specific answers, and when we are talking about literal life and death situations, clarity is crucial. The first time I asked the question, I was given the opportunity to practice asking it in a safe, risk-free training environment with nothing on the line, and even still, it brought tears to my eyes to say the words out loud. The question felt almost un-askable in a real-world scenario. Since then, I've ended up genuinely asking it far more times than I ever thought I would. Over time and with repetition, it has begun to feel a little more askable. And yet, when my wife Mendy asked *me* that question, I wasn't prepared for the flood of emotion that it would elicit.

As I mentioned in the opening chapter, my healing process on this trauma journey began in earnest the day I returned home from a hunting trip and decided to answer the un-askable question honestly. It was hard to get the words out, but I told her about what transpired on that boulder. I told her about the prayer. I told her about the unearthed trauma. I told her about the thoughts of suicide.

That day was November 7, 2021. We now celebrate November 7 in the Cummins household as "Stay Day," because that was the day I chose to *stay*—to not die by suicide—and accept the help and support that was being offered to me. Right up until the moment she asked that question, death by suicide felt like the only way out of the pain. The enemy had convinced me that I would never recover, and the pain ahead would eclipse what already felt unbearable. How would living be possible under the weight of it all? I'm glad I chose to stay. I'm even more grateful Mendy was willing to ask the hard question as a way of opening the door to vulnerability. Now, I have a deeper understanding of and appreciation for Isaiah 53:3, which describes our savior as, "A man of sorrows, acquainted with deepest grief" (NLT). Having been in the darkness myself, it now feels easier to step into it in order to point others who are there toward the light.

SUICIDE IN THE BIBLE

It would be natural if you were asking yourself right about now, "How does the topic of suicide play into our redemptive reversal of Ezekiel 34:4?" Simply put, we are called to seek the lost. Who is more lost than someone considering death by suicide as their only way out? Sometimes, the lost aren't wandering; they are drowning, and they need someone who isn't afraid to wade into the darkness with them and help bring them up for air. If you want an undeniably clear picture of God's heart for the desperately lost, take a moment to read Jesus' words in Luke 15.

I know the topic of suicide is widely taboo in many Christian circles, but it shouldn't be. After all, the Bible talks about suicide more than most people realize. We can't address what we aren't willing to discuss, so let's start our discussion on suicide by discussing the Bible—hopefully, that's an easy place to start for most of us. Before we jump into scripture, I think it's worth pausing for a moment to clarify some terms—a few of which we've already used and a few new ones that we'll see in the coming pages. (Note: you can find more key terms in Appendix C.)

- Suicidal Ideation → Active or passive thoughts of suicide stemming from a desire to end one's life. Passive thoughts may sound like, "I wish I wouldn't wake up." Active thoughts may include envisioning or considering specific means of death.
- Suicidal Desperation → Feeling like death by suicide is the only way out of a painful or overwhelming situation.
- Intrusive Thoughts of Suicide → Unwanted, involuntary thoughts, images, or impulses that may feel disturbing or out of character. Intrusive thoughts do not indicate that a person wants to act on them.
- Self-Harm / Non-Suicidal Self-Injury → Intentional self-inflicted harm (such as cutting or burning) used to cope with overwhelming emotional pain, but without the intent to die.
- Suicide Attempt / Non-Fatal Suicidal Self-Directed Violence → An act of self-injury with the intent to die that does not result in death.
- Death by Suicide / Die by Suicide → Sensitive language to describe a person's death resulting from self-directed violence with the intent to die.

At least five people die by suicide in the Bible:

- King Saul falls on his own sword in 1 Samuel 31:4 after being mortally wounded in battle to avoid a more gruesome death at the hands of his enemies.
- Saul's armor-bearer, likely overcome with grief and fear,

also falls on his sword in 1 Samuel 31:5 and dies by suicide along with King Saul.

- Ahithophel, King David's trusted counselor, hangs himself out of shame in 2 Samuel 17:23.
- Zimri, after a failed coup and being surrounded by his enemies, sets fire to the palace and dies by suicide in the flames in 1 Kings 16:18.
- Judas Iscariot, probably the most well-known suicide in the bible, hangs himself in Matthew 27:3-5 after being filled with remorse for betraying Jesus.[1] (We'll return to Judas' story in a moment.)

At this point, it might be easy to say, "Well, if those are the five people who for sure die by suicide in the Bible, that's not a very convincing list. All of those were *deeply* flawed individuals." Some might even say that some on the list *deserved* to die or that death by suicide might have been the honorable thing to do. It is worth noting that different cultures have different views on suicide as an honorable means of death in the face of dishonor. Also, it's hard to argue against these characters in the biblical narratives all being deeply flawed; they are! But are they any more flawed than other characters that we hold up as heroes? Was not King David, the man after God's own heart, a murderous adulterer?

What about other biblical heroes who don't have a recorded suicide attempt, but are clearly in a place of suicidal desperation?

- Job curses the day of his birth and longs for death in Job 3:11 and again in 3:20-22.
- Elijah, fleeing from Jezebel, reaches the point of exhaustion and emotional despair after isolating himself and asks God to take his life in 1 Kings 19:3-4.
- Moses pleads with God to end his life in a moment of feeling overwhelmed by the burden and pressures of leadership in Numbers 11:15.

- Jonah begs for death twice in Jonah 4:3 and 4:8 in his anger toward God.
- Jeremiah curses the day of his birth and laments that he didn't die in the womb and wasn't killed on the day of his birth in Jeremiah 20:14-18.
- The Apostle Paul claims in 2 Corinthians 1:8 that he and his companions were "so utterly burdened beyond our strength that we despaired of life itself" (ESV). It would be a stretch to say Paul was experiencing actual thoughts of suicide, but despairing of life is a dark place to be.
- I want to be equally careful not to conflate this dark, heavy moment with having thoughts of suicide—because clearly he didn't—but even Jesus in Gethsemane was so overcome by anxiety about what was to come that his sweat became like drops of blood, and he said to his disciples in Matthew 26:38, "My soul is crushed with grief to the point of death" (NLT). We'll come back to this moment for Jesus in chapter nine to look at the framework he gave us for managing such overwhelming emotions.

Honestly, the only key difference between this list and the list of those who died by suicide is that the people on the second list never engaged in any acts of suicidal self-directed violence. They let the page turn. In fact, I'm convinced that letting the page turn was the only difference between the ending to Judas' story and the ending for the *other* disciple who betrayed Jesus on the night of his death.

We don't usually categorize it in the same way that we think of Judas' betrayal of Jesus, but Peter also deeply betrayed Jesus that night. Certainly, I would feel deeply betrayed if someone I had poured into for three years had denied three times that they even knew me instead of standing by me in my darkest moment. Peter and Judas are both bitterly overcome with remorse and shame from their actions. Judas can't live with the shame and weight of knowing he betrayed Jesus to his death, and he ends his own life. And then, for most of us, on the *very next page* of our Bibles, Jesus is resurrected back to life. Peter let the page turn when Judas did not, and Jesus wiped away Peter's shame by reinstating him on the beach. Peter went on to be such a pivotal leader in the early church that it's hard to imagine what would have happened had he *not* let the page turn on his shame and had died by suicide alongside Judas.

And then we come to a much trickier biblical character to categorize: Samson. Not only is Samson painted as a hero in Judges 16, but he's also clearly held up as a hero in the Hall of Faith in Hebrews 11. And yet, by all accounts, it's hard for me not to categorize Samson's death as death by suicide, even though others would vehemently debate that categorization. My friend David would go as far as to question whether or not we should say that Samson's death was essentially a suicide bombing before there were bombs. I'll let you decide for yourself whether or not you're willing to go that far, but Samson's death by suicide certainly took the lives of several others as well. Regardless, here's what becomes readily apparent to me in looking over all of these instances of death by suicide and suicidal ideation in the Bible:

- The topic of suicide is not as simple or as clear-cut as many would have us believe. If the Bible doesn't shy away from sharing the depths of the emotional struggles of our biblical heroes, we shouldn't be afraid to talk about suicide or suicidal ideation either.
- Talking about suicide does *not* make it worse. In fact, I would argue that the biblical characters who are willing to clearly label their emotional despair to others or to God are the ones who survive. In many instances, we are able to see immense hope and flourishing in them after their moments of suicidal desperation, which gives hope to the hurting.
- Suicidal ideation is clearly not a sign of weak faith. Look at how some of our greatest heroes of the faith, like Moses, Elijah, and Jeremiah, struggled to know how to keep living given their circumstances.

- Go read each of those stories of those who let the page turn, and you'll notice that God doesn't condemn their despair; he engages it and provides for them.

Friends, if we are going to answer this call as shepherds to seek the lost, we have to be willing to step into the dark places as the hands, feet, and mouthpiece of Jesus to bring a message of hope. Again, my friend David would say, since we are temples of the Holy Spirit, we are *hope incarnate.* The presence of the Holy Spirit within us means we carry the presence of God everywhere we go. We carry love, healing, and hope everywhere we go. May we pray for eyes to see those who are lost and hurting and who need to experience hope in the flesh. And once we have seen, may we have the boldness and courage to step in and intervene.

SEEK THE LOST

The Good Shepherd himself came to seek and save the lost. We see his heart for lost and hurting people everywhere. His parables in Luke 15 reveal the heart of the Father toward the lost. His encounter with the woman at the well revealed his heart for the lost. In both Mark 5 and Luke 8, we see Jesus heal a demon-possessed, isolated, and destitute man engaged in regular acts of self-harm, and Jesus heals him at the expense of the livelihood of some local pig herders. Seeking the lost was Jesus' very mission. As spiritual shepherds, this, too, is *our* calling. Make no mistake, there is a clear call to seek the lost in terms of evangelism. Sharing the gospel with those who don't know Jesus is absolutely crucial to our mission and commission to make disciples. The good news Jesus preached, the gospel, was that the kingdom of heaven is near. Jesus defined his life and mission as the fulfillment of Isaiah 61 as he read it himself.

> The Spirit of the Lord is upon me, because he has anointed me to proclaim good news to the poor. He has sent me to proclaim liberty to the captives and recovering of sight to the blind, to set at liberty those who are oppressed, to proclaim the year of the Lord's favor.
> LUKE 4:18-19, ESV

We, too, are charged with seeking the lost by preaching the fulfillment of this gospel in the person of Jesus. For our purposes, in shepherding people through their mental health crisis, grief, and pain, it's important to again ask ourselves who is more lost than someone considering suicide as a way out? For whom is there more of a sense of urgency to declare hope, good news, and a message of liberation than those oppressed by suicidal desperation? These are the people who are in the most immediate need of a shepherd. I certainly needed a shepherd when I was at my lowest, and I'm grateful others showed up to shepherd me. Our calling, then, is to step in as the hands and feet of Jesus, and in order to help us know and remember *how* to step in, let's use the acronym **SEEK**.

Spot the signs
Evaluate the risk
Engage with empathy
Keep them safe

The acronym is simple enough to understand on its own, but let's take a look at each in greater detail.

Spot The Signs

A person in a place of suicidal desperation is almost always showing signs that they are not okay. They may not come right out and tell us they're thinking about suicide, but there are usually clues—small signals woven into their words, actions, or circumstances that let us know they might be thinking about suicide. Every evidence-based suicide intervention training I've experienced[2] agrees that someone dying by suicide without giving any prior warning is very rare. The real question isn't whether they're giving us signals; it's whether we're able to see the signs for what they are and have the courage to step in. When someone is hurting, they often communicate in lots of different ways. It can be in what they say, how they say it, or how they act. Let's take a look at a few different things to pay attention to.

First off, we want to listen for verbal cues. Words reveal what's happening beneath the surface. Someone in despair might not say, "I'm thinking about suicide," but they might say things like:

- "I can't do this anymore."
- "I just want to disappear."
- "Everyone would be better off without me."
- "I wish I could fall asleep and not wake up."

Even if they say it half-jokingly, don't brush it off. Anything with a tone of finality, hopelessness, or feeling trapped is a strong indicator that something deeper is going on. When people give verbal hints like these, they're often testing whether anyone will notice or care enough to ask a follow-up question.

Next, pay attention to behavioral cues. Behavior often speaks louder than words. Be alert for sudden or uncharacteristic shifts, especially if they point to withdrawal or preparation. Look for things like:

- Sudden and drastic changes in mood or appearance
- Giving away personal or valuable items
- Making arrangements for pets, belongings, or finances
- Saying goodbye in strange or final ways
- Pulling away from close relationships or community
- Risky or self-destructive behavior (substance use, reckless driving, unsafe decisions)

- Sudden and unexplained calm after weeks of distress. This may signal that the person has made peace with the decision to die.

These are not random actions. They often reflect an internal conclusion: "I can't keep doing this." The changes in behavior are almost always driven by some internal conflict or turmoil. A change in mood for a day can signal a hard day. A prolonged change in mood can be a sign that something much deeper is at play.

Finally, we want to pay attention to situational activators. Certain life events can intensify emotional pain and push a person toward the edge, especially when combined with feelings of hopelessness or shame. Common activators include:

- Major loss (death, breakup, job loss, divorce)
- Serious or chronic illness
- Financial or legal stress
- Spiritual crisis or disillusionment
- Embarrassing exposure of private sins, secrets, or shame
- Relational rejection or betrayal

The more of these signs we see stacking up, the more important it will be for us to pay attention to them. In the medical world, the phrase often used is, "When you hear beating hoofs, think horses instead of zebras." The implication is that the simplest explanation is most likely to be true. When it comes to signs of suicide, we want to be careful not to explain them away or ignore them, especially when multiple signs are giving us cause for concern. Someone experiencing a financial crisis won't necessarily end up in a place of suicidal desperation. Someone experiencing a financial crisis who is leaving short, handwritten notes of apology to those closest to them, and making arrangements for their pets, is much more cause for concern. As we spot the signs, let those signs act as an alarm bell to check in with the Holy Spirit and ask for discernment.

When I was in my own season of suicidal desperation, I tried my best to put on a brave face, yet those who knew me could tell something was wrong. Spotting the signs isn't about memorizing a checklist; it's about cultivating attentive compassion. People rarely hide because they want to be alone. They hide because they believe no one will come looking. Our job is to notice. To stay curious. To listen when others go quiet. Sometimes, the most Christlike thing we can do is pay attention to the signals that others are giving us, saying they are not okay. And when we spot the signs, we step in before it's too late. Did anyone come to mind while we went through that list of signs? It might be time to reach out to them.

Evaluate The Risk

Edwin S. Sneidman, in his book *The Suicidal Mind*, argued that suicide is less of a movement toward death and more of a movement away from pain.[3] I've heard many people echo the concept in their own words, saying something like, "It's not that I wanted to die, I just wasn't sure how to keep living." That was certainly reflective of my experience, that is, *until* Mendy asked me the hardest question she's ever asked in her life—the question that feels especially hard to ask a loved one. On some level, we know that as soon as the words are uttered, the moment becomes sacred because the question is inviting intense vulnerability. And yet, many people considering suicide are just praying someone will be willing to ask it. In other words, they are often hoping someone will give them a chance to release some of their pain.

Suicide survivor Kevin Hines talks about taking two buses to the Golden Gate Bridge the day he decided he was going to die by suicide.[4] He recounts being visibly distraught—openly weeping—and praying just one person would ask him if he was okay. Despite receiving several looks and even hearing multiple comments about how emotional he was, not a single person asked him if he was okay, so he jumped. It's heart-wrenching to hear Kevin say that the second after he jumped, he instantly regretted it and knew he had made the greatest mistake of his life, but it was too late. By God's grace, Kevin survived. In fact, he's on a very short list of people to survive jumping off the Golden Gate Bridge. Kevin is now a motivational speaker, sharing his testimony around the country and working in suicide intervention training.

Kevin's experience is not uncommon. In fact, studies have shown that approximately 7 percent of those who survived a suicide attempt eventually died by suicide, and roughly 70 percent of survivors had no further attempts.[5] What these numbers tell us is that our ability to help someone survive their initial moment of crisis *greatly* increases their chances of survival. It highlights how important it is that we be willing to straightforwardly ask people, "Are you thinking about killing yourself?"

When it comes time to ask the question, ask it very directly, but also calmly and kindly, "Are you thinking about killing yourself?" Leave no room for vagueness, because vague questions rarely get specific answers. Asking, "Are you thinking about *hurting* yourself?" could garner a response that doesn't let you know if they are considering suicide or struggling with other forms of self-harm or non-suicidal self-directed violence. Also, *how* you ask the question matters. Be careful not to phrase the question in a way that tells them you are all but begging them to say no by saying something like, "You're not thinking about killing yourself, are you?" That's not creating emotional safety, and it's barely an invitation for vulnerability. In fact, I'd go so far as to say it's a request for them to *avoid* vulnerability for your sake. It's saying that what they are dealing with is too much for you. Imagine saying, "You're not going to do something dumb, are you?" What a belittling way to phrase it. Instead, ask, "Are you thinking about suicide?" Or, "Are you thinking about killing yourself?"

It's natural to be hesitant or even afraid to ask that question. Not only is it weighty, but many people articulate a fear that if the person is *not* in a place of suicidal desperation, asking the question might plant the thought. Research by The National Council for Mental Health indicates the opposite to be true.[6] Their research shows that asking the question to someone who is not already experiencing thoughts of suicide does not plant the thought in their minds. What it *does* accomplish, however, is that if the answer is no, you establish yourself as a safe person who is willing to have a conversation about suicide in case that person ever does begin to have thoughts of suicide. You are earning the right to be heard.

In other words, asking the question not only saves lives, but it also increases emotional and psychological safety for the person you ask, because it establishes you as a potential lifeline should they need it down the road. I once asked the question and had someone convincingly say, "No." They later told me, "[Your willingness to ask the question] made me feel safe. If you were willing to talk to me about suicide, I knew it was safe to talk to you about any of my other struggles."

It's a heavy question to ask. It is a literal life and death situation if they say, "Yes." With that kind of weight attached, you don't want the first time you've said the words out loud to be in a high-stakes situation. It might sound weird, but it's something worth practicing. If you're comfortable, I'd like to invite you to pause for a moment and try it. Take a deep breath and say aloud, "Are you thinking about killing yourself?" If you're not in a place where you can do it (emotionally or physically), just whisper the word *suicide* aloud to get used to saying it. Take a moment to try it.

If you were able to join me in that exercise, I'd encourage you to take a few minutes to pause and breathe. What you just did might have been hard if you are worried about the safety of a loved one, and a specific face came to mind as you asked that question, but it also might have been your first step on a path that could save someone's life someday. It was very likely an emotionally taxing exercise, so take a moment to care for yourself. Go for a quick walk. As my friend Paris likes to say, "Touch grass," if you can. And if you yourself are experiencing thoughts of suicide, please call or text 988—just like you would 911—and someone will be there to talk to you, or check Appendix A for more resources. This moment is a semicolon in your life, not a period. Your story isn't over; there is more to be written, so reach out and let someone help you move toward healing in Christ. You aren't alone.

Engage With Empathy

It's okay to hope and pray their answer to the unaskable question is no. Wanting them to say no is just a sign that you care about their well-being. Of course, we don't *want* the answer to be yes, but what if we ask in a direct, calm, and inviting way and the answer is the dreaded yes? First off, take a deep breath, silently pray for the Holy Spirit to guide you and give you strength, and consider a response like, "I'm really sorry for the pain you're carrying, but thank you for trusting me with that information. You're not alone." This response is empathetic and caring, and it ensures you are there for them.

Once you have asked the hard question, the next step is to engage with empathy. Spotting the signs and asking the hard question matters, but what you do next could be life-saving. Your response doesn't have to be perfect; it just has to be present. Empathy bridges the gap between seeing pain and sharing it. It says, "You're not alone in this." That kind of presence can interrupt the downward spiral of shame, isolation, and despair that often drives suicidal thinking. Here's what it looks like:

1. **Lead with presence, not performance**. You don't need a script. You don't need to fix anything. You just need to show up. People in deep pain aren't looking for experts; they are longing for someone who will sit in the dark with them without turning on the spotlight too soon. Sometimes, the most powerful thing you can say is, "That sounds really hard. I'm so sorry you're going through this. I'm here with you. You're not alone." Empathy doesn't rush to rescue or reason—it remains. It listens. It slows down enough to let the other person feel seen.

2. **Practice active listening.** If they said yes to the hard question, they will almost always want an opportunity to share more about their pain or situation. Be careful not to make the situation about you. In many instances, people in places of suicidal desperation are looking for a release valve

for all the pressure that has built up inside of them. Simply asking the question and giving them a chance to share how thoughts of suicide became part of their story can be a huge help to them. Be attentive, show compassion, and show them visually and audibly that you are paying attention. Be careful not to hijack their story by sharing your own stories; that just makes the moment about you when what they need is to be heard. If it's helpful, go back to chapter one and revisit the section titled "Listen with Open Hands and an Open Heart" for tips on good active listening.

3. **Listen to Understand, Not to Correct.** When a person opens up, resist the urge to debate, minimize, or immediately problem-solve. Avoid saying things like, "You shouldn't feel that way," "You've got so much to live for," or "It can't be that bad." Even if meant kindly, those phrases can sound dismissive and deepen the sense of isolation. It might unintentionally communicate that they are weak because a stronger person wouldn't think their situation was so bad. Also, be cautious of asking unnecessary questions, especially avoiding questions that make you come across as voyeuristic. Any clarifying questions ought to be aimed at helping them clarify how they feel more than depicting a morbid curiosity, even unintentionally. Instead, practice reflective listening: repeat what you hear, validate the emotion, and ask gentle follow-ups. "It sounds like you've been feeling trapped and hopeless for a long time." "You're saying the pain feels unbearable, and you don't see a way out. Did I get that right?" This kind of listening communicates value: *You matter enough for me to slow down and hear your story. I see you. I'm with you.*

4. **Mirror the Heart of Jesus.** Throughout the gospels, Jesus models this kind of empathy. He sees and interacts with the bleeding woman that others ignore. He weeps with Mary and Martha before raising Lazarus. He touches the untouchable lepers *before* healing them. Empathy is not

weakness; it is the divine way of entering someone else's suffering. When you engage with empathy, you're embodying Christ's own presence, saying through your actions what Jesus says through the cross: "You are not alone. I'm not afraid of your pain. I'll stay with you."

- **Stay calm**—Panic communicates danger, not safety.
- **Stay near**—Physically or emotionally, don't let them drift into isolation.
- **Stay curious**—Ask open-ended questions rather than bringing judgment.
- **Stay kind**—Gentleness opens doors that fear closes.

When people reach the edge of hope, they often expect rejection or judgment. Empathy shatters that expectation. It creates sacred space for honesty, tears, and even anger. You may not have all the answers, but through your calm presence and courageous compassion, you can help someone begin to believe that life is still worth living. Because when we engage with empathy, we become living evidence that love still shows up, even in the darkest night.

Keep Them Safe

If you've invested in a suicide intervention training, this is where you will be grateful you did. You will have the tools to know exactly what to do next while you stay calm, cool, and collected. If you haven't attended a suicide intervention training, here's what I'd recommend: stop reading for a brief moment and save a few numbers as contacts in your phone. You don't want to be trying to remember where to find help when your head is already swirling from the weight of the moment.

I have multiple numbers saved in my contacts under names like "Suicide Help" and "Community Response Team," so they are easy to find in a moment of crisis. You can find local information with a quick internet search and then save those numbers. On the national level, you can just call 988. (It operates like 911, but for non-life-threatening mental health emergencies.) They will help you assess the situation and walk you through exactly what to do next. If you are worried about someone's immediate safety—as in, they have the means to harm themselves immediately accessible—call 911 instead. Aside from emergency numbers, you can also gather lists of Christian counselors as ongoing resources.

As spiritual shepherds, many of us will not have the tools to provide the right long-term care as the primary caregiver for someone in a place of suicidal desperation. We can be part of their support system moving forward, but our main role in this step will be connecting them with someone who can complete the intervention. It will be so much easier if you've done the work to gather a few resources before you find yourself in a real-life moment of crisis. If all else fails and you don't want to call 911, offer to take them to the hospital. Most hospitals will place them on a seventy-two-hour hold for psychiatric evaluation. This is not a long-term solution, but it can buy time to make a plan for what to do next.

Another thing to consider is asking what means they plan to use to die by suicide and working to remove access to those means. Consider this: women engage in suicidal self-directed violence at a rate nearly twice that of men,[7] and yet men who have an attempt are three to four times more likely to die by suicide.[8] Why do you think that is? Many suicide intervention organizations point toward means to explain these statistics: men are more likely to use a firearm as the means for their suicide attempt. Remember, only 7 percent of those who survived suicidal self-directed violence eventually died by suicide, and roughly 70 percent of survivors had no further attempts. This means, getting someone past the initial moment of crisis and helping them chart a course toward healing and recovery can make all the difference, because if they have an attempt and don't survive, we can't help them. Believe me when I say, I know exactly how passionate people can be about their guns, but if someone is in a place of suicidal desperation, removing access to lethal means for that season can be the difference between life and death. If you know someone is in a place of suicidal desperation, consider offering to help them get their firearms out of the house until they can get adequate help.

It will also be helpful to ask who may already be part of their support system and get permission to bring that support system up to date on what's going on. When someone is in a place of suicidal desperation, isolation is one of the greatest dangers. Safety increases when more than one caring person knows the truth. You might gently ask questions like:

- "Who knows you're struggling right now?"
- "Is there someone you trust that we could loop in together?" (NOTE: This should be a safe adult if you are talking to a student.)
- "Who has helped you get through seasons like this in the past?"

Especially for someone who lives with chronic thoughts of suicide, these questions can be incredibly important. They help uncover what has helped before—specific people, rhythms, places, or practices that brought stability or hope. Rather than assuming what they need, you're inviting them to help you build a safety net that's grounded in real life. If they're open to it, ask permission to reach out together. That might mean sitting with them while they make a call or send a text, or offering to be present when they share with a spouse, parent, close friend, pastor, or counselor. This communicates two powerful things at once: *you don't have to carry this alone,* and *your life matters enough to involve others.*

There may be moments when someone resists this idea out of fear, shame, or a desire not to be a burden. When that happens, respond with empathy, not pressure. You can acknowledge the hesitation while gently reinforcing the importance of shared care: "I hear that this feels hard, and I want to honor that. At the same time, having a few safe people aware of what's going on can make a real difference in keeping you safe. This is important."

Remember, your role is not to become their sole lifeline. In fact, trying to do so can unintentionally increase risk for both of you. Keeping someone safe often means widening the circle of care, not tightening it. When appropriate and with consent, helping activate an existing support system is one of the most loving and responsible steps you can take. Safety is rarely sustained by one person alone. It is strengthened through connection, shared awareness, and a community willing to show up together.

It's also worth noting that, if you are in a leadership position within a church (pastor, youth group, small group leader, child-care worker, etc.), you are likely considered a mandatory reporter. That means you are legally required to pass along information to the proper authorities if you have reason to believe a minor could be a harm to themselves or others. Talk to your church leadership about mandatory reporting details and processes; you'll want to make sure you know them.

Friends, the hard reality is that it's possible we can do everything right and still experience a negative outcome. I've experienced it. You can ask the hard question, sit with someone in their pain, connect them to resources, pray with them, and follow every step exactly as you've been trained, and still, someone may die by suicide because ultimately they have to be able and willing to accept the help we are offering. That grief is unlike anything else. It comes with a thousand what ifs, a heaviness that settles in your chest, and the haunting sense that you should have somehow known more, done more, or been more.

But hear me clearly: *you are not the Savior*. You are not responsible for outcomes that you cannot control. You are responsible for showing up faithfully, courageously, and compassionately, but you are not responsible for another person's final decision. Loving someone well does not guarantee their survival, and losing someone does not make you a failure. There is mystery here, and heartbreak, and a kind of sorrow that only the Good Shepherd can carry with you. And yet, even in the face of loss, your presence will have mattered. Your willingness to step in will have mattered. Your courage to ask the question will have mattered. Love is never wasted, even when it doesn't lead to the ending we prayed for. The Good Shepherd holds the stories we cannot fix, the lives we could not save, and the pieces of our hearts when they shatter. He is near to the brokenhearted, including you.

So, do not shrink back in fear. Do not let the fear of a painful outcome silence your voice or soften your courage. Keep showing up. Keep seeking the lost. Keep listening, asking, caring, and entering the dark places with the light of Christ. Faithfulness, not certainty, is our calling. And the Good Shepherd walks with us every step of the way. Your willingness to SEEK the lost increases the chances for a positive outcome, and that is always what we will pray for God to provide.

WE ARE ALL HERE

Engaging with someone who is in a place of suicidal desperation can undoubtedly be overwhelming. It's hard not to feel the weight of the stakes when it's literally a life-or-death situation. There is hopeful news backed by some encouraging stats, however. Research suggests that roughly two-thirds of people who experience suicidal ideation never engage in acts of suicidal self-directed violence.[9] A population-based study even found that only 7 percent of people with suicidal ideation attempt in the subsequent two years.[10] And as we've referenced repeatedly, it's also encouraging to know that of the people who survive suicide attempts, 70 percent of them never have another attempt. These statistics speak to the importance of timely intervention so that healing can be found. Believe it or not, we actually see an example of this play out in scripture.

In Acts 16, Paul and Silas are confronted by a mob in Philippi for sharing the gospel. They are attacked, stripped, beaten with rods, and thrown into prison. Decidedly, not a good day for Paul and Silas.

Around midnight Paul and Silas were praying and singing hymns to God, and the other prisoners were listening. Suddenly, there was a massive earthquake, and the prison was shaken to its foundations. All the doors immediately flew open, and the chains of every prisoner fell off! The jailer woke up to see the prison doors wide open. He assumed the prisoners had escaped, so he drew his sword to kill himself.
ACTS 16:25-27, NLT

First off, can we pause for a second to recognize that even after having been stripped, beaten with rods, and thrown into jail, Paul and Silas are still praising God? What an incredible testimony of their faith and the presence of the Holy Spirit strengthening them. This is powerful, so don't miss it. Now, imagine the desperation of the jailer. In his mind, having lost the prisoners meant shame, disgrace, losing his job, and maybe losing his family in the process. Spotting any signs there? Not seeing a way out, he draws his sword, but look at what Paul does next.

But Paul shouted to him, "Stop! Don't kill yourself! We are all here!"
ACTS 16:28, NLT

I don't know about you, but if I had just been stripped, beaten, and thrown into jail and then God provided a miraculous way out, I would have been *running* out of that jail toward freedom! Instead, Paul leans in. He sacrifices the guarantee of his earthly freedom so the jailor might experience spiritual and emotional freedom. Paul meets the jailer right in his darkest moment, stepping into his deepest pain with him. I encourage you to read for yourself what happens next. Not only is the jailer's life saved, but so are the souls of his entire household. The jailer, his family, and his servants all accept Jesus and are baptized into the faith. Talk about a turn of events.

Friends, what if people all around us heard us crying out in one voice as God's church, shouting, "STOP! DON'T KILL YOURSELF!

WE'RE ALL HERE!"[11] What if the hurting and lonely, the lost among us, knew that they aren't alone, and that we are willing to walk alongside them on their path to healing and hope? Sadly, no demographic is immune to thoughts of suicide, and deaths by suicide happen at alarmingly high rates in our country. According to Soul Shop Suicide Prevention Training, one in four people has experienced suicidal thinking at some point in their lives, but has likely never talked about it due to shame or embarrassment.[12]

We need more safe places for people to express their despair. We need more people willing to step down into the darkness with those who are hopeless. We need more shepherds willing to seek the lost. Jesus left the ninety-nine to pursue the one. Will you?

SELF-CARE AND REFLECTION

Friends, I want to emphasize the importance of proper self-care after the emotional toll this chapter likely took on you as you read. Please take some time to connect with Jesus and allow the Holy Spirit to strengthen you today before moving on. Reach out to a trusted friend, mentor, or spiritual shepherd, and let them tend to you for a bit. If you are feeling unsafe, check Appendix A for resources. You're not alone.

Today, I will care for myself and stay connected to God by:

Space for Reflection:

THREE

ROUND UP THE STRAYS

He gathers the lambs in his arms and carries them close to his heart.
Isaiah 40:11

THE WOLF PACK

Depression is like a ninja; it often sneaks up on you, so you don't see it coming. In fact, I never would have used the words *depression* or *depressed* to describe how I felt my senior year of college. Mental health was rarely, if ever, talked about back in the mid-2000s, so I doubt any of my friends would have used that language either. But those closest to me could tell I wasn't okay. And yet, I think my season of depression snuck up on them just like it snuck up on me.

By this point in college, my best friends and I had affectionately begun referring to ourselves as *the wolf pack:* made up of Aaron, Eric, Jeff, DiFab, and me. At some point toward the end of our senior year, we even bought ourselves what we called *wolf pack tags.* But let's be honest, they were friendship bracelets. I wore mine for years after we graduated from college until it was ripped off on a rafting trip. The bracelet—I mean wolf pack tag—meant so much to me because the friends it represented meant so much to me. They still do.

45

We did just about everything together in college. I even lived with two of the four of them at different points, so suffice it to say, we knew each other exceedingly well. And yet, because depression is a ninja that no one sees coming, it took a while for the signs to add up enough that they could tell something was off for me. Just like a sheep that absent-mindedly strays from the flock, it rarely happens all at once or in ways that are abundantly noticeable until the sheep is just gone.

It started with mental distancing. I would be in the same room with them, but struggle to focus on the conversation or activity. I'm sure I simply came across as distracted at times. Then, it slowly progressed to emotional distancing. I found myself saying unkind things to them and immediately shaming myself for being so unkind, though it rarely led to an apology. I didn't realize it, but I was crying out for help. Then came the social distancing—and not the COVID kind. I would stay in my room playing games on my computer for hours *if* I could drag myself out of bed at all. I just didn't have the energy to be around anyone.

Now and then, I would show up as my old self, but those days became fewer and farther between as the depression worsened. The truth is that I wasn't a good friend in that season as I pulled away. I was an even worse roommate. I will be forever grateful that the wolf pack treated me like a paper sheep in that season.

PAPER SHEEP

My friend and co-laborer in Christ, Jonathan, introduced me to the concept of *paper sheep* in the fall of 2025. The idea is simple enough: if a shepherd has one hundred sheep but can only count ninety of them at the end of the day, well, that shepherd has ten paper sheep. On paper, they have ten more, but those ten sheep have wandered off at some point throughout the day. A good shepherd will always go looking for those ten paper sheep. Our Good Shepherd always does.

If a man has a hundred sheep and one of them wanders away,
what will he do? Won't he leave the ninety-nine others on the
hills and go out to search for the one that is lost? And if he
finds it, I tell you the truth, he will rejoice over it more than
over the ninety-nine that didn't wander away! In the same way,
it is not my heavenly Father's will that even one of these little
ones should perish.
MATTHEW 18:12-14, NLT

People in seasons of deep anguish, pain, and mental health struggle
will rarely disappear all at once. It's far more likely that they will pull
away slowly over time until they don't have the energy to show up
anymore. Maybe you already know all too well the quiet ache of
watching someone drift away, not knowing what to do. Maybe you've
been that straying sheep. I began to distance myself as a direct result
of the depression, but sheep stray for lots of reasons. As shepherds, we
are called to pursue the paper sheep in our lives and round up the
strays if we are going to live a redemptive reversal of Ezekiel 34:4—
easier said than done. Perhaps you also already know what it's like to
walk on eggshells around someone because it seems like, no matter
how hard you try to help, your attempts seem to make things worse.
Join the club. So, how do we round up the strays as people begin to
emotionally, spiritually, and socially withdraw? And, better yet, how
can we do it in a way that doesn't make things worse?

ROOM TO WANDER, GRACE TO RETURN

Jesus reveals the heart of God the Father toward strays through what
is perhaps his most famous parable. In Luke 15, Jesus shares the
parable of the prodigal son. Because of this parable, we often think of
a prodigal as someone who wanders away only to return after
reaching the end of their rope, but the word *prodigal* actually means
wastefully extravagant. In Jesus' parable, the son who strays demands
his inheritance early, goes away, and lives a wastefully extravagant,

prodigal life—at least until his resources run out. In my experience as a pastor, there are, indeed, plenty of strays who wander away looking for an opportunity to sow their wild oats or are lured away by the things of this world. Charles Spurgeon said it this way, "You will never know the fullness of Christ until you know the emptiness of everything else but Christ."[1] Plenty of sheep begin to stray, looking for fulfilment in all the wrong places.

And yet, there are also plenty of strays who begin to wander, not because they are lured away by the things of this world, but because they are hurting or overcome with shame. Some have experienced church hurt—sometimes from people who were trying to help and ended up making things worse. Sometimes, they wander from exhaustion, disillusionment, or disappointment. Some people stray when they don't feel safe enough to be honest. Others, when they feel unseen, misunderstood, or judged. Some strays are doing their best to protect themselves from deeper hurt or from collapsing in on themselves because the anguish from a loss is too great, and they can't bear having to put their pain into words (more on this in the next chapter).

Regardless of what sent the strays wandering, Jesus gives a clear picture of what God the Father's response is the moment the stray turns back for home. In Luke 15, the father of the prodigal gives his son room to wander, but also grace to return.

> But while he was still a long way off, his father saw him and was filled with compassion for him; he ran to his son, threw his arms around him and kissed him. "The son said to him, 'Father, I have sinned against heaven and against you. I am no longer worthy to be called your son.' But the father said to his servants, 'Quick! Bring the best robe and put it on him. Put a ring on his finger and sandals on his feet. Bring the fattened calf and kill it. Let's have a feast and celebrate. For this son of mine was dead and is alive again; he was lost and is found.' So they began to celebrate.
> LUKE 15:20b-24

The father's response in this story is staggering. What if the paper sheep in our lives knew this was the kind of homecoming they could look forward to? What if they were confident that they would be met with grace, love, and support rather than judgment, shame, and a demand for penance? What if we gave them a glimpse into the heart of their heavenly Father? Perhaps we could if we were to adopt the three postures of the father from this story.

He sees him coming a long way off because he's been long awaiting his return. The father has been keeping a weather eye on the horizon, day after day, longing for the moment he would see his son crest the hill on his return journey home. This is a posture of *eager watchfulness*. The father is so overcome with joy at the sight of his son's return that he can't wait for his son to make it home. He runs out to meet him while he is still on his way. This is a posture of *joyful pursuit*. And then the father initiates a celebration, brushing aside the son's well-rehearsed monologue of contrition. This is a posture of *lavish grace*.

A POSTURE OF EAGER WATCHFULNESS

There are a few things we can surmise from the father's posture of eager watchfulness if we are to adopt the same posture. First and foremost, the very fact that the father had been keeping a weather eye on the horizon meant he had not lost hope that his son would return. It can be hard to carry a constant burden for the paper sheep in our lives. After all, when our hope peaks and we think we see them cresting the hill, but it turns out the shadow on the horizon isn't the stray returning, it can activate a whole new season of grief. And yet, Paul encourages us in Romans 8:25, saying, "But if we look forward to something we don't yet have, we must wait patiently and confidently" (NLT).

Our hope is not in the outcome. Our hope and confidence are placed in Christ. It is placed in the comfort of knowing that our heavenly Father loves the strays even more than we do, as hard as that might be to imagine. And that leads to the second element of this posture: not only do we hope, but we also practice patience. We must not lose a sense of urgency to do our part as the Holy Spirit leads, and yet for most of us, the issue is not moving too slowly; the issue is a lack of patience. Remember, strayed sheep wander for all sorts of reasons. If their wandering comes from a place of deep hurt, lament, or anguish over a significant loss, patience is needed all the more. We cannot rush someone in their grief, and God is not afraid of their lament—look at the entire book of Lamentations for proof. We have evidence that the opposite is true, as we see Jesus weeping with those who weep (more on that in the next chapter). If we can learn to trust God's heart for the strays and keep our hope alive, we can do our part by interceding on their behalf in prayer.

I know the father in this story represents God the Father, but as an earthly father, I can assure you that if it were me, I would seek to be vigilant in prayer as I daily scanned the horizon. I certainly hope we, as shepherds, would not underestimate the power of prayer. In so many ways, I felt sustained during my trauma journey by the prayer warriors in my life, like my mom and Flo.

Flo was an elderly lady at our church during our time in Florida. She would always introduce herself, saying, "I'm Flo White, like Snow White." Every single time I saw Miss Flo, she would give me a big kiss on the cheek, take both of my hands in hers, and as tears streamed down her cheeks, she would say, "What you do is so important, and I pray for you every single day."

Please believe me when I say that Flo's impact on me was profound beyond what I could put into words—to the point that, even though she had already passed away when I was going through my season of trauma therapy, I still felt strengthened by Flo's prayers. I count her as one of my greatest allies in ministry and life, and I look forward to getting another kiss on the cheek from Flo someday in glory. Depending on the circumstances, we may not always feel free to let our paper sheep know we are praying for them, but please, fervently pray for them nonetheless. It may feel like we are not doing enough, but true, enduring intercessory prayer is the most powerful thing we can do for anyone.

Outside of prayer, there are other practical ways we can adopt a posture of eager watchfulness. First off, be like Motel 6 and leave the light on for them. Leaving the porchlight on as a sign of welcome is doing something that maintains small, gentle contact points without pressure. Maybe it looks like sporadic texts that are not shaming or guilting, but aimed at letting them know we are thinking of them. Something like, "Thinking of you and praying for you today." Or, "Saw something today that made me think of you. I hope you know how loved you are." These texts are just enough to let them know the light is on for them to come home without pressuring them to step back into relationship.

For me in college, it looked like wolf pack members DiFab and Aaron inviting me to go get a honey-butter chicken biscuit at midnight without turning it into an interrogation. It looked like Jeff keeping us stocked up on habanero-flavored Doritos and whole milk —our weird snack combo of choice—so I would feel seen and loved. It looked like Eric inviting us all to Taco Bell and then asking Aaron to drive so he wouldn't have to, which always made us laugh. Clearly, I was very food-motivated in college.

Eager watchfulness might look like modeling a non-anxious, peace-filled presence that creates space for someone's pain. Your calm presence might create the safe horizon they will eventually steer toward. Modeling this will require some of us to become more comfortable with silence. I am naturally wired to be comfortable with silence, but I have plenty of friends who struggle sitting in silence with other people, and I understand why. Silence is something that must be sought in our day and age. It must be *practiced*.

Eager watchfulness might look like little acts of kindness or service that do not veer into enabling territory. These small acts can make a big difference in making someone feel safe, seen, and cared for. Things like sending a gift card to their favorite restaurant, dropping by with essentials, or doing a chore on their behalf. Get creative and look for things that will speak their specific love language if you know it. And I know we already covered it, but just for good measure, bathe all of these acts of kindness and service in prayer.

We do, indeed, need to be careful not to enable others to avoid doing the work of healing that is theirs to own. Acts of kindness or service don't remove responsibility; they encourage it. I've found that when a stray begins to relate to us as though they are entitled to our care, attention, or emotional labor, it may be a sign that we've slipped from shepherding into rescuing or enabling. In those moments, our presence may unintentionally protect them from taking the next courageous step toward healing. Healthy shepherding walks *with* people, but it does not walk *for* them or *prevent* them from walking. We offer compassion, support, prayer, guidance, and community, but we cannot do their healing work on their behalf. Boundaries aren't a withdrawal of love; they are an invitation to agency, growth, and ownership.

Even Jesus, the Good Shepherd, never forced healing or chased someone into maturity. He asked questions, invited participation, honored agency, and allowed people to choose whether they wanted to be well. We see this in John 5:6 when he asked the lame man, "Would you like to get well?" That same posture keeps us from enabling. We stay near, we cheer them on, we pray, and we support, but we also leave room for the Holy Spirit to do what only he can do.

A POSTURE OF JOYFUL PURSUIT

Joyful pursuit looks like active, compassionate, and intentional engagement with the strays, meeting them halfway. It communicates that we don't expect them to come all the way back on their own; we will go out to meet them and journey with them on their way back. If they aren't ready to come back to church, it's okay because we can meet them for coffee. If they aren't ready to reenter into community, it's okay because a smaller contingency of community can hang out on their terms. If they aren't ready to talk, it's okay because we're comfortable sitting in silence.

That's what Jeff often did for me during our senior year. I didn't always have the energy to talk, but if I at least mustered the energy to come out of my room, he'd be content to play the *Guitar Hero* video game or watch our favorite TV show *Heroes*. At times, he'd be content to sit in mostly sweaty silence as we ate our latest bag of habanero Doritos and our mouths burned with sweet, spicy pain. Those were his versions of seeing me a long way off and coming out to meet me on the return journey, and it created psychological safety as I came out of my season of depression.

Rounding up the strays with a posture of joyful pursuit might mean showing up consistently and patiently, even if they don't reciprocate right away. At the very least, it does not seek to shame with any version of sarcasm. I remember once being greeted with a snide, "Well, look who decided to grace us with his presence!" I can assure you the comment did not make me want to show up in that space again. Here's a thought: maybe let's not punish the very behaviors we hope to see. What would have made me want to show up again would have been something more along the lines of, "It's really good to see you," or "We really appreciate the effort," or anything that encouraged the behavior again without resorting to sarcasm or manipulation. Tone matters in these instances. Even the right words can be misinterpreted if said in the wrong way. In the wrong tone, even words like "We miss you" can come across as intending to mean "You're disappointing us." As long as we bathe our words in grace and compassion, we pray our hearts will be conveyed as we convey the heart of the Father.

It is also interesting that the father of the prodigal son didn't *demand* contrition, and yet he did not interrupt his son as he offered his contrition. Once the son was done with his contrite monologue, the Father didn't directly reply to him, but he *did* address it. The son claimed he didn't deserve to be called the father's son anymore, and look what the father said to the servant in Luke 15:24, "This son of mine was dead, and is alive again" (ESV). A posture of joyful pursuit is quick to remind the strays how we see them and how God sees them —as his children. It doesn't demand a heartfelt apology before reengagement, and yet it makes space if the stray wishes to offer one.

There is something powerful in giving space for others to offer a statement of repentance without dragging it out or expecting it. Just showing up might be the best apology they can give. Notice and rejoice over small acts of reengagement as a means of positive reinforcement. They might be doing the best they can, and according to Jesus, that ought to trigger a party.

A POSTURE OF LAVISH GRACE

Lavish grace is celebratory love that silences shame for the stray. It is an opportunity to mark their return with warmth and joy. It's a reinstatement into relationships, and it clearly states that they belong. If strays thought this is how they would be greeted, I think more people would seek to make amends and reenter the fold.

I am not suggesting that in pursuit of lavish grace we bow to entitlement. When others show up with a posture that *expects* grace, or manipulatively *demands* grace, well then, it's not really grace anyway. In that instance, setting a healthy boundary might be the best thing we can do for our sake *and* theirs. If someone is demanding to be taken back without owning the pain they caused, that is not us pursuing them; that's them attempting to manipulate us. But if we are truly seeking to pursue and round up the strays as shepherds, well then, lavish grace will feel healing for both parties.

We see Jesus hold all three of these postures with Peter in his restoration on the beach that we talked about in chapter two. When the disciples returned from their fishing trip, Jesus was already waiting on the beach with a posture of eager watchfulness. Not only was Jesus waiting, but he was already cooking breakfast for them in joyful pursuit. Finally, he reinstated Peter gently with lavish grace, erasing Peter's three denials with three opportunities for Peter to affirm his love for Jesus. Jesus himself acted as the father for the prodigal Peter, reminding us how he waits patiently for us to run back to him after our failures while also modeling how we can do the same as we round up the strays.

SHEPHERDING THE NINETY-NINE

Jesus showed us the heart of the Father to leave the ninety-nine and seek the one. That heart is powerful. It's bold. It's comforting. It's worth emulating because it's a huge part of the culture of the kingdom. The ninety-nine still need shepherding, too, though. I don't highlight this as a way of letting the posture of the older brother sneak into our thinking, but as a way of reminding us that sometimes the ninety-nine will need help knowing how to bring the straying sheep back into the fold. I'm not just talking about a church context here, either. The fold can look like a group of friends, a family, or any other host of contexts for community.

Sometimes, the ninety-nine will have been hurt by the straying sheep's wandering. Sometimes, there will be resentment toward the lost sheep—a sure reflection of older-brother-syndrome. And sometimes, the strays are straying *because* of the ninety-nine. I'm not sure if you've recognized this to be true, but not every follower of Jesus is a perfect reflection of their Savior all the time. If you can't feel the intended sarcasm oozing out of that line, go back and reread it in the tone and accent of a stereotypical valley girl. Of course, we know this to be true. This will require both grace on the part of the straying sheep and correction on the part of the shepherd to protect that vulnerable sheep.

Regardless of the circumstances of the one sheep's straying or the part the ninety-nine may or may not have played, it shows greater care on the part of the shepherd to prepare the ninety-nine for the straying sheep's return. The ninety-nine have a role too. When one sheep returns, it's the whole flock's rejoicing that makes the Father's joy visible. A community that celebrates restoration more than perfection becomes the safest place for healing. That kind of community will not happen without intentionality from the shepherd.

So, keep your eyes on the horizon, but don't forget the hope that fuels your watching. The Good Shepherd is already at work in the hearts of the strays, calling them home even as he whispers courage to you to keep looking, keep praying, and keep loving. To round up the strays is to walk in step with the Good Shepherd himself. It's to live with arms open wide, ready to embrace those who come limping home and to remind them—again and again—that they still belong. Helping them *feel* like they still belong will likely require some shepherding of the ninety-nine as well. And when you, the shepherd, and the ninety-nine alike, rejoice at the sheep's homecoming, heaven will rejoice with you.

THE HEART OF THE FATHER

I've said it already, but it's important to remind ourselves that our pursuit of the strays is a way that we can reflect the heart of the Father. The father didn't just welcome the prodigal back; he redefined what welcome means. To shepherd like him is to wait with eyes wide open, to move with joy instead of judgment, and to throw a party when grace wins. Maybe it's worth thinking about what our response would be if one day our strays responded to our pursuit and decided to come home to relationships that are waiting eagerly.

Maybe we would do well to remember the words of Anne Lamott as she reflects on the grace of God, saying, "I do not at all understand the mystery of grace—only that it meets us where we are but does not leave us where it found us."[2] Remembering the woman caught in adultery that we mentioned in chapter one, may we recognize that we may one day be given the chance to be the mouthpiece for grace by meeting the strays right where they are. We will love them too much to leave them there, but we may not get the chance to walk them toward healing if we do not first meet them in grace.

Again, it's worth praying for the heart of the Father to become your heart. To pray for wisdom to know how to pursue the wandering paper sheep. To be willing to say, "We *have* to go round them up . . . because they are ours . . . because they belong . . . because it's what the Good Shepherd would have us do." Pray, too, for perseverance and resiliency because sometimes it's years before the paper sheep return home. So, keep a weather eye on the horizon. Bathe them in interceding prayer. Leave the light on by reaching out regularly so the connection is not severed completely. Because one day, a paper sheep you've been watching for will crest the hill. And when they do, you'll want to be the first one running.

57

SELF-CARE AND REFLECTION

Today, I will care for myself and stay connected to God by:

Space for Reflection:

FOUR
BIND UP THE INJURED

THERE ARE NO WORDS

There are few things more disorienting than being startled awake in the middle of the night in a bed that isn't your own in a room you don't recognize. One of the most healing things for my soul after my traumatic brain injury was getting to finish a cycling event with my sister Cristina on the one-year anniversary of my accident. It felt good to accomplish something so big on the same bike that took so much away. It was redemptive. It was life-giving. And it launched me into a whole new world of road cycling where I regularly participate in large group, long-distance events.

It was one such cycling event that led me to the unfamiliar bed in a strange room, as I slept in a rented basement suite the night before an event. When I awoke to the sound of my phone ringing, I was so startled and disoriented that it took me a lengthy beat to realize where I was and what was happening. Then, I saw the name on my ringing phone, my heart skipped a beat, and my stomach fell like the bed had dropped out beneath me. I knew what I was about to hear before I even answered the phone.

For well over a year, I did my best to support a dear friend as he did everything he could to prevent his son from sliding deeper into a hole of mental illness. For months, my friend had openly shared his concern for his son's safety as the mental illness progressed. I prayed with him and his wife for their son's safety. I offered support as best I could. I tried to give advice from my mental health and suicide prevention training. And yet, despite all of their efforts to provide him with help and assistance, their son was unable to accept it. In chapter two, we talked about how people have to be willing to accept help, and that we can't do the work for them. I was about to learn how true that is.

On the other end of the phone, my friend was calm, and yet I could feel the pain and disbelief bubbling beneath the surface of his words as he told me the tragic news of his son's death by suicide. There was a catch in my breath, and my voice cracked as I mustered the only words I could think of: "I'm so sorry." That's all I said. That's all I *could* say. Because in moments of utter anguish, there are no words. I didn't sleep the rest of the night under the weight of sharing their grief. The next day, during the cycling event, I spent far more energy praying for my friends than I did focusing on my riding.

It was three days later when I got to sit with my friend and his family in their home and grieve with them in person. Once again, I said very little in my time with them. We hugged. We cried. I listened. We hugged some more. It was an honor to sit with them in their grief, but it was also hard to witness it up close.

By the time I got to my car, my strength was gone, and I broke down. The enemy tried to tell me what a failure I was for not being a better friend. For not being a better pastor. He tried to convince me that just about anyone would have done a better job consoling my friends. Once again, the enemy's lies can be pretty convincing, echoing in our heads. But then, in the midst of that storm of shame, the Holy Spirit graciously reminded me of Job's friends.

HIS SUFFERING WAS TOO GREAT FOR WORDS

To say Job had a bad day would be an understatement. It's more like he was leading the pack in a competition no one wanted to enter to claim the prize for worst sequence of events ever. Virtually all at once, Job lost every good thing in his life—his wealth, his home, his family, and his health. And then, to top it all off, Job's wife poured salt into his open wounds by essentially telling him, "You might as well curse God and kill yourself, Job." This is decidedly not a good spouse move.

But then, in the midst of all that pain, all that suffering, and all that anguish, something beautiful happened.

> When three of Job's friends heard of the tragedy he had suffered, they got together and traveled from their homes to comfort and console him . . . When they saw Job from a distance, they scarcely recognized him. Wailing loudly, they tore their robes and threw dust into the air over their heads to show their grief. Then they sat on the ground with him for seven days and nights. No one said a word to Job, for they saw that his suffering was too great for words.
> JOB 2:11-13, NLT

There are a lot of lessons to learn from Job's friends if we want to answer the call as shepherds to *bind up the injured.* For our purposes, we will talk about binding up the injured as being present with people in moments of crisis. The word *crisis* refers to a time of intense difficulty, danger, or emotional upheaval that demands an urgent response. It's often a turning point—a moment when the direction of a person's life, health, or situation could drastically change for better or worse. We can think *big* with things like the loss of a loved one, losing a job, getting divorced—the list could go on.

But we should also be careful not to dismiss things that we would deem as *little.* Losing a pet, having to drastically reduce or change expectations, or not getting a promotion might seem small in the grand scheme of things, but they can still trigger a need to grieve.

Even small things can feel massive if someone is already carrying a lot of weight, is under a lot of pressure, or is struggling with their mental health. Think of it this way: it only takes a small pin-prick to pop an overfilled balloon.

When we bring on new small group leaders into our student ministry, I try to remind them that we don't get to determine the intensity of a student's pain. We might have the life experience and perspective to know they will be fine tomorrow after getting dumped by their girlfriend of two hours, but just because it might seem small and insignificant to us, it doesn't mean it doesn't feel earth-shattering to them. There is a thin line between helping by offering perspective and coming across as dismissive, so proceed with an abundance of caution when trying to offer perspective. I can't imagine anyone feeling tempted to diminish what Job was going through. Regardless of our perceived scope, size, or scale of the crisis that the person across from us is experiencing, Job's friends provided a pretty great framework to follow when being present with someone in their moment of crisis.

First off, Job's friends *showed up.* Don't underestimate how powerful it is that Job's friends heard about his crisis, and their immediate reaction was to say to one another (in the subtext), "We *have* to go be with him." They were willing to be interrupted. They dropped everything and traveled to be with Job, which was certainly disruptive to their normal rhythm. The truth is, showing up for people in the midst of their crisis will almost always be disruptive for us in some way. It will cost us something—be it time, energy, attention, etc. And yet, Job's friends paid the cost to drop everything and were willing to be interruptible in order to be present with Job at his lowest moment. Are we willing to be interruptible? Are we willing to linger with people who are hurting?

Job's friends also *joined Job in his grief.* They didn't try to draw a silver lining onto the black smoke pall that covered Job. They didn't say, "Well, you might have lost all of your children, but at least you still have your wife." They didn't say, "Cheer up! Things can't get any worse." Nor did they say, "Let's go blow off some steam in Nineveh to get your mind off of things." Instead, they let him see through their actions that his grief was appropriate, and they joined him in it. In the Bible, tearing one's clothes and covering one's head with dirt or ashes acted as a visible signal to others that someone was in a deep place of grief and despair. They felt it was *helpful* for people to know their emotional state. In our day and age, it seems like grieving is expected to be done in private. Countless times, I've heard people praise others for being "strong" in their grief (i.e., refraining from emoting in a way that would make others uncomfortable). Very unintentionally, we treat grief or pain like a sickness that we are worried about catching, so with comments like that, we unknowingly thank others for not forcing us to face our own emotions.

Not only are *our* emotions completely appropriate in a grieving situation, but showing our emotions gives others permission to show their grief as well. Emotions expert (yes, that's a thing) Brené Brown recalls a conversation with grief expert (also a thing) David Kessler, "Each person's grief is as unique as their fingerprint. But what everyone has in common is that no matter how they grieve, they share a need for their grief to be witnessed. That doesn't mean needing someone to try to lessen it or reframe it for them. The need is for someone to be fully present to the magnitude of their loss without trying to point out a silver lining."[1]

One of the greatest gifts we can give someone who is experiencing any sort of deep-seated pain or grief is to appropriately join them in it. Counterintuitively, it actually *helps* them on their healing journey. Grief will not leave us until we've allowed ourselves to feel it. To sit with it. To welcome it for a season rather than avoiding it. Brown also shares a quote by Robert A. Neimeyer, "Most people who struggle with complicating loss feel a great pressure to 'tell the story,' to find someone willing to hear what others cannot, and who can join them in making sense of the death without withdrawing into awkward silence or offering trite and superficial advice regarding the questions it poses."[2] Are we willing to show up and sit with others in their grief, bearing witness to their pain? It might be the most healing thing we ever do for someone.

Finally, Job's friends recognized the depths of his suffering—that it was too great for words—and they responded appropriately with *silent presence*. For the longest time, one of the biggest reasons I was so reticent to show up for others in their pain was because I didn't know what to say. The summer after the freshman year of my degree program in theology and ministry, I had a great-uncle pass away. My dad was particularly close to this uncle, so the news was hard for him. I remember the discomfort of not knowing what to say to my dad was enough that the thought of entering the living room where he was crying on the couch induced a mountain of anxiety.

My mom encouraged me to go comfort him, and when I was resistant, she said, "Tomy, you're studying to be a pastor." The implication being that if I couldn't sit with my own dad in his moment of pain, how would I be able to do it for others? It was a big moment for me because, as childish and naive as it may sound, I didn't realize what I was signing up for by studying to be a pastor. I had been focused more on dodgeball and camp than on pain and grief. It took virtually every ounce of resolve I could muster, but I went and sat next to my dad on the couch and said the only words I could think of: "I'm sorry." I'm sure you're noticing a recurring theme for me when faced with the grief of others.

My dad took a deep breath and spent the next several moments recounting his favorite memories of his uncle. By the end of the fairly one-sided conversation, I noticed that he had stopped crying. I think I was too young to understand the power of what had happened that night, but looking back, I get it now. My dad didn't need me to fix anything or take the pain away. He needed me to be present and to witness his grief while giving him space to process. This is the power of what Job's friends did for him: they showed up, they joined him in his grieving, and they recognized that presence speaks more powerfully than words.

The Holy Spirit reminded me of these truths as I wept in the car after sitting with my friends in the anguish of their son's death by suicide. It will never feel like we are doing enough, but showing up, joining others in their grief, and saying more with our presence than we do with our words is a beautiful picture of what it looks like to bind up the injured in moments of crisis.

DESCRIPTIVE, NOT PRESCRIPTIVE

This moment with Job's friends is, in my opinion, the most beautiful moment in Job's entire narrative. They truly provided a shining example of how to be present for someone in the darkest moments of their life. Until, that is, Job's friends broke the silence, and everything went south in a hurry. In no time at all, Job's friends began heavily implying, if not outright accusing Job, that Job brought suffering upon himself by sinning.[3] At one point, they even went as far as telling him his children *deserved* death![4] Job even called them out for it in chapter 16, verse 2, saying, "What miserable comforters you are!"

They twisted Job's words, became more concerned with defending their theology than caring for their friend, and turned to fear and shame instead of comfort and empathy. I suppose one bright spot for Job's friends was that it appeared they were well acquainted with Proverbs 25:20, which says, "Singing cheerful songs to a person with a heavy heart is like taking someone's coat in cold weather or pouring vinegar in a wound" (NLT). They didn't try to bypass Job's grieving by trying to cheer him up, which, according to Solomon, is never a good move, but they also didn't get it right, did they? This portion of Job is certainly meant to be descriptive, not prescriptive, so please don't follow their example past Job chapter two. And surely, we'd never get it *that* wrong, but the truth is, trying to give simple and pat answers to complex feelings of grief and pain will always do more harm than good.

On one hand, it's hard to blame Job's friends for not remaining silent. After all, Job was the one who broke the silence when he began to pour out his grief and ask some truly difficult questions. Like Job's friends, we won't always have good answers to those hard questions. And be wary of, like Job's friends, *thinking* we have good answers to hard questions when, in actuality, our answers are just shaming or reductive. Instead, I believe we are far better off affirming their pain and pointing them to what we do know.

We know God isn't afraid of our pain; he is near to the broken-hearted and binds up those whose spirits are crushed. We know God isn't afraid of our questions—just look at the book of Lamentations or the many psalms of Lament. And we know our God is in the business of bringing good out of bad situations. We see that happening from cover to cover in the entire redemptive arc of humanity from the fall in Genesis to the new creation in Revelation. We may not be able to speak with authority about the hope of a given situation, but we certainly can speak as agents of hope. As a temple of the Holy Spirit, you are hope in the flesh. You get to show up as a carrier of the presence of Jesus to the hurting. So, how did Jesus show up for the hurting?

JESUS WEPT

When his friend Lazarus died, Jesus knew full well what was about to happen. Jesus knew that in a matter of minutes, they would be hugging and rejoicing that Lazarus was alive again. He knew those mourning would receive the ultimate comfort of getting to see their friend and brother alive again, and still Jesus wept.[5] Note that it doesn't say, "Jesus dramatically shed a single tear," or "Jesus quietly cried with the greatest of dignity." No, it says, "Jesus wept." As in sobs, contorted facial expressions, and maybe even a little snot. This was an ugly cry because that's what weeping looks like. But why? Would it not have been better to be a pillar of strength for those present? Had Jesus forgotten for a moment that they would be enjoying a post-resurrection snack with Lazarus within the hour? Why does he weep when he already knows the outcome?

Scholars have come up with a wide array of answers to this question. And it makes sense: grief is complicated. N.T. Wright, in his book *John for Everyone*, argues that Jesus wept out of righteous indignation at the broken state of creation that is marred by sin and death. Others like St. Augustine of Hippo would say it has more to do with

Jesus being brokenhearted at the unbelief of the mourners. I resonate with Frederick Bruner, who wrote, "I think *'bawling'* fairly captures Jesus' genuine heartbreak with and compassion for those around him."[6]

Whatever we may resonate with about the *why* of this moment, here's what we can observe: Jesus does not chastise those who are grieving; he joins them. He gives those present a visual reminder of Psalm 34:18, "The LORD is close to the brokenhearted; he rescues those whose spirits are crushed" (NLT). Jesus is revealing the heart of God and setting the ultimate example of how to bind up the injured: be present with them in their darkest hour and join them in grieving. Before healing, there is holding. Before words, there is weeping.

Jesus' actions in this moment are antithetical to the posture of many people today. In a culture where others are praised for a lack of emotion, where grief is treated like a communicable disease that we are afraid of catching, and where grief is viewed like a mirror that we are terrified to look into, the example of the Good Shepherd beckons us upstream into a posture of presence and compassion. For Jesus, the thought of choosing not to help someone when he could do so filled him with righteous indignation.[7]

The Apostle Paul explicitly expounded on the example of Jesus with the command to "weep with those who weep,"[8] because together as one body, "If one part suffers, every part suffers with it."[9] For some of us, sitting with people in their pain is so second nature that it feels silly that it needs to be explicitly commanded. For others, it might be one of the scariest and most unnatural commands in scripture. Whether it feels like common sense or a wildly challenging proposition, it's good to be reminded of what we said in the last section: as a temple of the Holy Spirit, you are hope in the flesh. In these holy and heavy moments, we can learn to rely on the Holy Spirit to do the heavy lifting *through* us.

Certainly, none of us has the emotional capacity to carry everyone's grief *for* them, but that's not what Paul was saying. In their book *Boundaries*, Dr. Henry Cloud and Dr. John Townsend point to Galatians 6 as a great clarification for the extent of our role. In this passage, Paul commanded us in verse 2 to "Carry each other's burdens, and in this way you will fulfill the law of Christ." Interestingly, Paul, in seeming contradiction, then also said in verse 5, "For each one should carry their own load." So, what is happening here? Is Paul speaking out of both sides of his mouth?

Cloud and Townsend point out the crucial difference between the words *burden* and *load*. "The Greek word for *burden* means 'excess burdens,' or burdens that are so heavy that they weigh us down. These burdens are like boulders. They can crush us. We shouldn't be expected to carry a boulder by ourselves! It would break our backs. We need help with the boulders—those times of crisis and tragedy in our lives. In contrast, the Greek word for *load* means 'cargo,' or 'the burden of daily toil.' This word describes the everyday things we all need to do. These loads are like knapsacks. Knapsacks are possible to carry. We are expected to carry our own. We are expected to deal with our own feelings, attitudes, and behaviors, as well as the responsibilities God has given to each one of us, even though it takes effort."[10]

The point they are making is that we cannot do personal growth work for others, nor can we carry their grief, trauma, or pain *for* them. But we can carry it *with* them. Or, perhaps, to some extent, we can be used by God to help carry *them*.

WWSD—WHAT WOULD SAM DO?

Perhaps my favorite character in J.R.R. Tolkien's entire *The Lord of the Rings* epic is Samwise Gamgee. Sam is a faithful friend who supports Frodo every step of the way on Frodo's journey from his home in the Shire to Mount Doom deep in the heart of Mordor. If you're sniggering at me or rolling your eyes right now, it's okay; I get it. I'm a proud nerd. A hobbit standing at just three feet, six inches tall—an impossible hero—Frodo is asked to carry the one ring—an impossible burden—deep into enemy territory so it can be destroyed—an impossible task.

If you've read the books or watched the movies, you are likely well aware that Frodo would have never come close to completing his task or have been able to bear the crushing weight of this burden without Sam's support. Toward the end of their journey, Frodo finally found the end of himself and couldn't go on by his own strength, so in a moment of epic heroism, Sam (referring to the one ring) says, "I can't carry it for you, but I can carry you!"[11] Sam literally slings Frodo over his shoulder and begins carrying Frodo and the ring up the mountain. I still get chills thinking about it. Of course, the better question is always, "What would *Jesus* do?" But from time to time, when I'm walking with people through hard seasons, I ask myself, "What would Sam do?"

The burdens of others are not our burdens to carry for them. We would get crushed ourselves if we were to try. And if you are naturally wired to be a helper and a giver, you likely already know this from the painful experience of trying. While it's not biblical to carry the burdens of others for them, there is indeed biblical precedent for helping carry others in their need, or at the very least, prop them up. Sam dramatically carrying Frodo up the mountain is, in my mind, a great biblical allusion to Exodus 17.

In verses 8–16, the battle of the Israelites with the Amalekites is outlined. Moses' strategy in this battle was to stand on a nearby hill and hold up his staff over the battle as the Israelites fought the Amalekites. Weird choice, Moses. On the surface, it seems nonsensical that their military strategy for such a key battle would be to simply hold up a walking stick, but remember what that staff represented to the Israelites: God's presence and favor.

Good grief, what if that was our strategy in *every* battle? What if our constant reminder to ourselves in the midst of hard moments is that God is *with* us and that God is *for* us? My bad, Moses. Turns out, it's a pretty great tactical advantage. And here's the kicker: it works! As long as Moses' arms were up, holding up the representation of God's favor and presence over the battle, the Israelites were victorious. But, as Moses got tired and lowered his arms, the Amalekites gained the advantage. Seeing this, Aaron and Hur channeled their inner Samwise Gamgee and held up Moses' arms *for* him. Anachronisms aside, there is yet another great lesson to learn here for how to bind up the injured in moments of crisis. So, how do we practically hold up the arms of others who are trying to hold up a reminder of God's presence and favor over their battles?

LOVE ASSERTIVELY

With the best of intentions, when friends or loved ones are walking through difficult trials, people often offer, "Let us know how we can help." I've used that phrase more times than I can count. The heart behind the phrase is pure and empathetic. The problem with it is that it puts yet another burden onto someone who is already tremendously burdened: the burden of coming up with a way we can help them. Had Job's friends offered such an open-ended statement, I'm fairly certain Job would have had no earthly idea what to ask for, given the turmoil he was experiencing. The question is too tactical and *in the weeds*. Emotional turmoil makes it hard, if not virtually impossible, for most people to think tactically or to notice details. I still think a loving, open-ended offer to help is immensely valuable. The details and weeds of life will eventually be pressed in upon them, and knowing they have someone who is willing to help with those details can ease the burden. The open-ended offer is powerful as long as it is accompanied by something else: assertive love.

Mendy and I have been tremendously blessed over our many years of full-time, vocational ministry to be on the receiving end of the assertive love of others. When we lived in Florida, I had to have an emergency appendectomy on the same day that we had an ultrasound to find out if our firstborn would be a boy or a girl. Picture me doubled over in pain in a chair next to Mendy while she lay on a table with gel on her belly. Then, picture our OBGYN doctor announcing that we were having a girl while simultaneously side-eyeing me with a look of grave concern. On the plus side, Mendy and I both have pictures of our insides from the same day!

It is a long story for another book as to why it took so long, but it was hours later, after midnight, when they finally rushed me into emergency surgery to remove my appendix. Despite the late hour, no fewer than five of our closest friends and coworkers came to check on us, rushing in before the surgery to pray for us. One of our best friends, Christina, sat with Mendy late into the wee hours of the morning during my surgery. All told, I was in the hospital for less than twenty-four hours, and yet we had fifteen visitors. The following week, Mendy didn't have to cook a single meal thanks to the collective efforts of the Millses, Kellys, Greens, Lindseys, and a host of other friends. One of our favorite families from our student ministry, the Williamses, came and mowed our overgrown half-acre lot, which took over two hours! None of these people asked; they simply showed up, found ways to help, and loved assertively.

Many of us have likely had experiences of people showing up and loving assertively during a medical crisis or the loss of a loved one. But where are the casseroles when someone's season of anxiety is crippling? Where are the lawnmowers when someone's bout of depression makes it feel impossible to get out of bed? Where are the offers to sit up with someone late into the night when they are overwhelmed by thoughts of suicide? Mendy and I have experienced the assertive love of others in all of those situations as well, and we are beyond grateful. Sadly, I think it's rare to have people show up in a mental health crisis in the same ways we show up for others in a physical health crisis. It shouldn't be so rare—it *wouldn't* be if we started taking seriously the call to bind up the injured.

I couldn't begin to list all of the ways people showed up for us during the summer of 2022 as I went through my intensive trauma therapy. The texted prayers of Bob, Doug, Gary, and Stephen. The felt prayers of Beth, Mom, Cristina, Tim, and other prayer warriors. The texts of encouragement from the Wolf Pack and the Unclers. The yummy meals provided at the table at Nancy and Gene's, not to mention the daily handwritten notes of encouragement and the unparalleled care packages of Nancy. The many security team members from our church who mowed our lawn each week. The grace of Mendy's managers at Compassion International, who told her to simply do her best at work in the midst of a hard season. The chance to feel normal at a taco joint with Ryanne and J Witt. The extra burden of carrying the weight of leadership for our student ministry from the seat of an admin by Jenna. The innumerable nights of "sitting in the suck" in the pergola of safety with Tay and Ste. The days on end of caring for our children by Jenna and Taylor, Taylor and Stephen, and family. The list could go on for pages. To all of you: a simple "thank you" could never capture the gratitude that we have for how you loved us assertively during that season. I'm here to write this book because of you.

We live in an age of silent suffering. It is slowly getting better, but in many contexts, mental health and suicide still carry significant enough stigma to keep people from asking for help. In this age of silent suffering, the power of assertive love is an X Factor. We can exponentially multiply psychological and emotional safety for others by showing up as the hands and feet of Jesus to care for others when we love assertively.

Who around you is lost and hurting as they walk through a moment or season of extended crisis? How could you show up for them practically today or in the coming week? Pick a few options from the list below, and love them assertively as you either begin or strengthen this habit in your life.

- Send a text or, better yet, drop off a hand-written note or send a voice memo so they hear your voice. Do it again tomorrow. And the next day. And the next. A lot of people start strong and then lose steam, causing those who are hurting to feel forgotten.
- Make a meal or buy a digital gift card for their favorite food delivery service.
- Bring some groceries.
- Ask when would be a good night to take their kids out for the evening, so they can have some time to themselves.
- Ask if it would be okay to pick up their dirty laundry, so you can wash and fold it for them.
- Ask what night of the week would be best to come tidy their house.

- Offer to help complete any unfinished projects at work or around the house.
- Bring them a puzzle, LEGO set, or something that would feel like a fun, therapeutic activity.
- Buy a comfort gift like a weighted blanket, candle, cozy socks, etc.
- Buy or make a visual reminder of God's work and presence in their lives, like a *kintsugi* bowl.[12]
- Invite them out for tacos and, unless they bring it up, just have fun and give them a chance to be reminded that normalcy still exists. If they say no, ask again next week. And the next. Find the line between pestering and persistence, because even though they weren't ready this week, maybe next week they will be. The average bout of depression can last months.
- Put key dates on your calendar and contact them on the anniversary of difficult days.
- Speak hope over them when they've forgotten how to hope for themselves.
- Offer to help with the details of funerals.
- Offer to pick them up and drive them to hard appointments or meetings.
- Send a daily prayer or scripture reminder of the truth of God.
- When you're with them, opt for, "Can I pray over you now?" instead of, "I'll be praying for you."
- Make an affirmation list of the good you see in them to remind them how others see them and how God sees them.
- Fast on their behalf and seek God for them.
- Send a meaningful worship song that makes you think of them, or make a playlist that you've curated just for them.
- Encourage counseling or support groups, or other resources, without shame.

- Give them permission to say no to things that are too much right now.
- Advocate for them in a boundary-honoring way by speaking up on their behalf if you see others trying to help in ways that are harmful.
- Leave notes of encouragement and love on sticky notes in places they will find them later.
- Invite them to serve alongside you at a volunteer opportunity.

I pray this list will get your creative juices flowing as you seek to love assertively. The more personalized and thoughtful the act of assertive love, the more seen, valued, and cared-for your loved ones will feel. The storms of life will come for us all. Loving assertively will, in some small way, tell the hurting person that when the waves are roaring, they can be reminded that the Lion of Judah also roars. But before he roars, he'll weep with them.

SELF-CARE AND REFLECTION

Today, I will care for myself and stay connected to God by:

Space for Reflection:

FIVE

HEAL THE SICK

Daughter, your faith has made you well. Go in peace. Your suffering is over.
Mark 5:34, NLT

WHO AM I?

"Who am I if I can't preach?" Two different seasons of depression in my life have hinged on this very question. The first came in 2009 after being let go from my first full-time job in ministry. I first felt drawn into full-time vocational ministry in the eighth grade as I got to know Travis—my student pastor from seventh grade all the way through high school, and his influence on my life was profound. Somewhere between all of the fart jokes and original songs about ponderosa snags, he taught me how to be like Jesus. Maybe I was called to do the same for others? I spent my high school years wrestling with the idea of ministry before finally deciding in my final semester of high school to go to Southern Nazarene University to study theology and ministry.

My four years at SNU were incredible. They were also pockmarked with seasons of struggle. I didn't recognize it at the time, but I already mentioned in chapter three that my senior year as a ministry major and ministerial intern was fraught with depression. So far, it's the earliest extended season of full-blown depression that I can recognize. I rarely showered. I barely made it to classes. I missed so many required chapels that I received the maximum monetary penalty for chapel fines—a special mark of shame for ministry majors. That season of depression was marked by difficult questions and identity struggles, but even with all of the pain and turmoil, I somehow made it through to graduation. Not long after graduation, I was hired into my first full-time ministry role as the high school pastor at a church in Broken Arrow, Oklahoma.

A low-grade underlying depression followed me into that first full-time ministry job, bubbling underneath the surface of everything I did. Despite that, I also experienced a renewed hope. Maybe God could use me in ministry after all. I started thinking maybe I *was* wired to help students on their journey of spiritual formation after a solid year plus of questioning it. Things were looking up one day, one flag football game, one night of hitting raw eggs with a golf club in the parking lot of the church, one prank on the girls during their lock-in, one spicy wing challenge at a time. Then, after six months of trying to find my footing, the ground fell out beneath me. Our lead pastor, who hired me, moved to a church in Florida, and I had no idea of the storm that would follow.

In short, the multiple months of transition and the heightened sense of instability they brought were exhausting. Once we finally found a new lead pastor, in his first month or so after being hired, he was forced to let multiple staff members go because the church could no longer afford to pay everyone. I was one of them. Looking back, I don't envy the financial crunch he inherited or the tough decisions he was forced to make. They were very kind as they let me go. They spoke truth over me, saying how much they believed in me and wished they didn't have to make the decision. Still, after years of pursuing God in ministry, I was devastated. I questioned so many things. Why would God let this happen after I had been so faithful to follow him? Was the enemy right? Was I not cut out for ministry? If so, who am I if I can't preach? Like Napoleon Dynamite, I didn't have any good skills.

I was hired on as an employee of my alma mater (SNU) in the admissions office thanks to the good word my mentors, Blair and Tollya, put in for me. They knew me well after three years of interning and working for them, but the problem was that I was currently a shell of the intern and employee they had known prior. I only lasted about six months in the admissions office, and I'm fairly certain that I added virtually nothing to the team during that season. As I wrestled with my identity and calling into ministry, I continued to struggle with all of the familiar depression symptoms I had before. I was constantly late. I missed so many days that my paycheck was docked more often than not. When I could drag myself out of bed, I regularly sat in my office watching TV shows on my laptop because I couldn't find any motivation to work. I cringe when I think of the hit to their reputation that must have come after Blair and Tollya put their neck out for me. I can't help but cry when I recognize this was the state I was in when Mendy and I got married in the middle of that season because, clearly, I was far from living as my true self. I wasn't the man she deserved me to be.

I spared SNU from having to fire me by quitting before they could drop the axe. As I mentioned in chapter one, the look on my boss's face was one of pure relief when I quit. All of the pain, turmoil, and depression stemmed from that singular question, "Who am I if I can't preach?" I never had time to find the answer in that season because just a few months later, Mendy and I moved to Florida, where, after a short stint as the director of our sports ministry, I again became a high school pastor. Things slowly got better as I settled into my calling once again.

I wouldn't be forced to wrestle with the question of my identity again until after my cycling accident. The first time I tried to preach a few weeks after the accident, while the aphasia was still at its worst, it was brutal. I spent most of my time bumbling as I couldn't find the right words I was looking for. My thoughts regularly trailed off as I would forget what I was saying mid-sentence. It was incoherent, and the confused looks on the faces of the football team that I was preaching to let me know it.

I rushed home and wept after the experience. Not only from sheer embarrassment, but from fear. The day prior, my neurologist told me that brain injuries are tricky. It could be months before symptoms subsided—*if* they ever did. Was this what the rest of my life was going to look like? Would I ever be able to string multiple sentences together without significantly stumbling over my words? Would I be able to preach again? I spent weeks crying out to God, asking for healing. In the true spirit of lament, I complained to God as I again questioned my identity. I felt abandoned, and yet I kept crying out and seeking God in the midst of my pain. And then one night, as clear as a bell, I felt God saying to me, "Don't you realize that if you never preached another sermon in your life, I wouldn't love you any less? You are my son, and I love you for who you *are*, not for what you *do*."

IMAGO DEI

It would be a grand oversimplification to say all mental health struggles stem from the singular struggle of identity issues. Mental health struggles are complex issues that often stem from social, emotional, and physiological factors, as well as spiritual. Most of us, as spiritual shepherds, are unqualified to speak with authority to the social, emotional, and physiological elements, and we would be wise to recognize those limitations and encourage whole-person care by professionals who can speak with authority in those areas. And yet, as carriers of God's Holy Spirit, we *are* uniquely qualified to speak to the spiritual element.

So, again, be reminded that identity dilemmas are not the sole cause of mental health issues, especially not in cases of diagnosable mental illnesses. That is certainly not the case, and yet in my own experience of working with others on their mental health journeys, I would say it's often an underlying factor. At the very least, it's a wildly common issue in our culture today. We are constantly bombarded with messages from people, companies, and politicians who have an ulterior motive in trying to shape our sense of identity. As a result of so many voices vying for large slices of our identity pie, we are facing an epidemic of people who feel unknown, unseen, and unsure of who they truly are.

Even as Christ-followers, we are prone to spiritual amnesia, where our God-given identity is buried beneath layers of cultural noise and propaganda. False gods try to label us with false names until we no longer know who we are, what we are worth, or where to find truth. This confusion of identity leaves us vulnerable to every voice but God's. We are shaped by platforms more than purpose. Image more than the *imago dei*.[1] As spiritual shepherds, this might be our opportunity for greatest impact: helping others see and root their identity in Christ. To speak the truth louder than the enemy is speaking lies.

To this end, we must start by recognizing that healing isn't primarily about addressing symptoms. As pastor and author Steve Carter would say, it's about addressing "the thing beneath the thing."[2] Too often, we think of healing solely in terms of *getting better*—as in, the symptoms going away—but biblically, healing is way more about *being made whole.* A whole identity knows *who* they are because they know *whose* they are. Having a healthy sense of identity is about seeing yourself rightly, knowing you're loved, and living free from the lies that grow in the dark. In other words, an identity rooted in Christ starts in the mind. It starts with orthodoxy—right thinking—before it can impact orthopraxy—right actions. This is the entire premise of Dallas Willard's powerful work, *Renovation of the Heart.* Willard's profound book seems aimed at further unpacking Jesus' most direct words to the Pharisees about inside-out transformation.

What sorrow awaits you teachers of religious law and you Pharisees. Hypocrites! For you are so careful to clean the outside of the cup and the dish, but inside you are filthy—full

of greed and self-indulgence! You blind Pharisee! First wash the inside of the cup and the dish, and then the outside will become clean, too.
MATTHEW 23:25-26, NLT

Willard's framework, like Jesus' words, points to transformation, starting inside before progressing outward through our actions. Scripture, too, seems to be intent on going out of its way to make sure we understand that true transformation starts in the mind.

Don't copy the behavior and customs of this world, but let God transform you into a new person by changing the way you think.
ROMANS 12:2, NLT

Those who are dominated by the sinful nature think about sinful things, but those who are controlled by the Holy Spirit think about things that please the Spirit. So letting your sinful nature control your mind leads to death. But letting the Spirit control your mind leads to life and peace.
ROMANS 8:5-6, NLT

Throw off your old sinful nature and your former way of life, which is corrupted by lust and deception. Instead, let the Spirit renew your thoughts and attitudes. Put on your new nature, created to be like God—truly righteous and holy.
EPHESIANS 4:22-24, NLT

We take captive every thought to make it obedient to Christ.
2 CORINTHIANS 10:5b

Fix your thoughts on what is true, and honorable, and right, and pure, and lovely, and admirable. Think about things that are excellent and worthy of praise.
PHILIPPIANS 4:8, NLT

Since you have been raised to new life with Christ, set your sights on the realities of heaven, where Christ sits in the place of honor at God's right hand. Think about the things of heaven, not the things of earth.
COLOSSIANS 3:1-2, NLT

You will keep in perfect peace all who trust in you, all whose thoughts are fixed on you!
ISAIAH 26:3, NLT

Search me, O God, and know my heart; test me and know my anxious thoughts. Point out anything in me that offends you, and lead me along the path of everlasting life.
PSALM 139:23-24, NLT

I could go on. Scripture compels us to focus on controlling and surrendering our thought life because it affects every other part of our lives. As whole persons, every bit of us is impacted when we begin to root our identity in Christ rather than in the lies of the enemy. Healing happens when lies lose power, and the truth is finally allowed to speak at full volume. That truth—the truth of our identity in Christ —doesn't directly address symptoms of depression, anxiety, suicidal ideation, grief, etc., but it will most definitely make a significant impact on the symptoms. "Healing the sick" in Jesus' ministry almost always involved more than just physical change; it included emotional, spiritual, and communal restoration. For our purposes, healing the sick will be a focus on helping others root their identities in Christ and helping them learn to speak truth over themselves louder than the enemy speaks lies over them.

INFIRMITIES, INIQUITIES, AND IDENTITIES

It's hard to miss that healing was a major piece of Jesus' earthly ministry. We have account after account of Jesus healing sickness, blindness, paralysis, and even reversing death. He healed infirmities, iniquities, and identities alike; in many instances, all for the same person. When Jesus healed the man born blind in John 9, he not only healed the man physically, but he also restored him socially by rejecting the idea that he had been made blind because of his sins or the sins of his parents. This is a deeper transformation of identity as Jesus removes shame, restores dignity, and invites purpose.

Imagine being given such a label as a child, being told from your youngest age that you can't see because you're a sinner. Even after he was healed, the Pharisees tried to double down on this label in John 9:34, saying, "You were born a total sinner!" I have to imagine that after this life-changing interaction with Jesus, however, the Pharisees' words didn't stick to the man any longer. Sadly, for many of us, these labels *do* tend to stick. We begin to believe the lies of the enemy. People walking through hard seasons are often carrying lies that are defining their realities and shaping their identities.

- "I am too broken."
- "I'm a burden."
- "I'm not enough."
- "My mental illness defines me."
- "God is disappointed in me."
- "God doesn't love me—others maybe, but not me."
- "The world would be better off without me."

When lies like these take root, they can be difficult to uproot. They begin to shape our identity. It's why we see Jesus modeling the power in understanding that healing doesn't come solely from treatment, but from truth as well. And certainly, it's not an either/or, but a both/and. And the capital "T" truth begins with who God says we are.

When the woman with the issue of blood in Mark 5 secretly touches the hem of Jesus' garment, she is physically healed in an instant. Jesus, feeling power go out of him, stopped and called her out —not to shame her, but to restore her identity. In a powerful moment that reshapes her entire identity, Jesus called her "Daughter." After years of being emotionally, socially, and physically outcast by her community, Jesus restored her identity with a label of intimacy and belonging. She came looking for relief and instead received restoration.

This is what Jesus offers each of us: to redefine and reshape our identity by leading us to anchor it in him. After all, Jesus changed Simon's name to Peter, which means "the rock," long before Peter was stable and mature. Jesus did this because he is more concerned with who we are becoming than with who we have been. Jesus proclaimed this over Peter in Matthew 16:18, saying, "Now I say to you that you are Peter (which means 'rock'), and upon this rock I will build my church, and all the powers of hell will not conquer it" (NLT). Interestingly enough, Jesus used two different words for rock in this statement. He started by changing Simon's name to Peter, *petros*, which means "a small, movable stone or even pebble." He then said on this rock, *petra*, he would build his church. Petra (apart from being an incredible classic Christian rock band) is a far more stable rock, like a large boulder or bedrock.

Many theologians, exegetes, and apologists have pointed out the play on words that Jesus was making. They highlight that Jesus was calling Peter the small stone, petros, and calling the confession and statement of faith made by Peter the actual bedrock, petra, of the church, rather than saying Peter himself would be the bedrock of the church. I understand the distinction, but I believe Jesus was *also* prophetically speaking into Peter a truth about who he would *become* by the transformational power of the Holy Spirit at work in him. Again, speaking this prophetic truth over Peter set the course that Peter would follow, and this moment reshaped his identity. In the same way, I believe Jesus wants to reshape our identities by healing our infirmities and removing our iniquities as he sets us on a new trajectory.

For each of us, our role to play in our own healing journey is one of continual surrender. Jesus, through the power of the Holy Spirit, does the heavy lifting on this healing journey as we participate in the divine collaboration, but only if we work to surrender the old labels in favor of replacing them with the truth of who God says we are. As we shepherd others on their journey, we can't do the surrendering for them. What we *can* do is support them as they do the work of identifying the lie that creates the label, and then continually speak the truth that will dissolve the label until only truth remains.

WHERE DO YOU WALK WITH A LIMP?

At a communicator's summit, we were asked the question, "Where do you walk with a limp?" I immediately knew the context of the question. In Genesis 32, Jacob physically wrestles with God, and two things are forever changed for him after that encounter. First, Jacob's name was changed to Israel. As we just discussed with Simon's name being changed to Peter, the name change also represented a change in direction. It is God speaking truth into and over Jacob's life to give him a new identity. Secondly, however, it changed how Jacob walked —literally. Jacob's encounter with God changed his identity, but it also forced him to walk with a limp.

Those of us who have done our own work of replacing lies with truth know what it means to walk with a limp. I can definitively say my own identity work has left me walking with a limp as I've wrestled with God. In so many ways, I think it's the limp itself that equips us for the kind of shepherding work we are talking about. For years, I would sit with a student who was experiencing significant pain, and yet I would feel so ill-equipped to know how to show up for them. Like I said in chapter one, my heart would be breaking for them, but my only response would be akin to a metaphorical pat on the head from a distance as if to say, "You poor thing . . . bless your heart," like a patronizing southern grandma filled with pity. I wanted so badly to help and be present with them, but I couldn't get past the invisible wall that separated us.

I don't feel that invisible wall anymore. My trauma work destroyed the wall. It's one of the reasons I wouldn't trade the experience I gained during my trauma journey despite all of the pain that came with it. That's not to say that I now know how to perfectly show up for everyone every single time. Believe me, I am far from perfect, and I still get it wrong, but I no longer feel the overwhelm that comes from feeling ill-equipped. My healing journey left me walking with a limp, but it also equipped me. I don't know if you even caught it in the previous paragraph, but I said that my heart would break *for* them. Now, my heart breaks *with* them. I think that's one of the key differences between pity and compassion. Pity creates distance. Compassion creates presence. It allows us to draw nearer to the pain of others because we've faced our own pain and lived to tell the tale.

So, I ask you the same question I was asked at that communicator's summit: "Where do you walk with a limp?" That limp might be your second greatest superpower. Remember from chapter one that our first greatest superpower is the Holy Spirit, who, again, does the heavy lifting but often uses us as part of that heavy lift. Your limp—the work you've done to replace the lies and labels from your past with the truth of God so you can live out of your identity in Christ—is the very thing that will equip you to help heal the sick. It makes you more like Jesus, who was described as "A man of sorrows, acquainted with deepest grief."[3]

I once heard Christian hip-hop artist Lecrae say, "We should never be ashamed of our scars because our scars are proof that our wounds have been healed."[4] Interestingly, we often think of the pain associated with our physical scars rather than sitting in wonder at the healing they represent. I look at the scars I bear across four of my fingers (two on each hand) and am reminded of the pain and panic I experienced as a child when those fingers got pinched in the metal hinges of the folding chair that I had just sat in. It was awful. I sat there in excruciating pain, unable to call for help for several seconds as the pain and fear paralyzed me. (Until this very moment, however, I don't think I've really thought often enough about what a miracle it is that God designed my body to heal itself as represented by these scars on my fingers.)

I often look at the scar on my daughter's upper lip and shiver as I'm reminded of the blood that poured out of her lip after she was bitten by a dog and had to get stitches. I kept myself together emotionally as I held her hand in the hospital, but the second I climbed into bed that night, the dam broke, and I wept from the emotion of the day. Sometimes, it's still painful to look at Laney's scar as it brings the emotions flooding back, but more often than not, I now look at that scar and am reminded of how brave and calm she was the entire day as the Holy Spirit filled her with peace. That makes me cry for different reasons.

If you're not familiar with the Japanese art form of *kintsugi*, I would encourage you to do a quick internet search to find some pictures. Kintsugi is an art form by which artists take broken pieces of pottery and repair them with gold. In kintsugi, the imperfections are the very thing that makes the bowls, pots, and mugs more valuable and beautiful. As we are healed by Christ, we, too, become like kintsugi. The healing and repair that is brought to our lives become the very ways we can glorify God.

The same scars in our lives can represent both pain and healing, and we shouldn't be ashamed of those scars. It's the scars in Jesus' hands, feet, and side that proved to Thomas that Jesus had both died and been resurrected back to new life. The scars surrounding our identity can and should similarly represent the ways that we have died to ourselves—the old lies and labels of the enemy—and how we have been raised to new life in Christ. Paul told us that, "Anyone who belongs to Christ has become a new person (other translations say "new *creation*"). The old life is gone; a new life has begun!"[5] The scars we bear from the old life that is now gone might be the very thing that equips us to be used by the Holy Spirit to aid others in their transformational journey as they learn to live as new creations themselves.

LESS LIKE A LIGHT SWITCH, MORE LIKE A SUNRISE

Pastor John Mark Comer talks about this process of uprooting lies in favor of anchoring our identities in Christ as learning to *Live No Lies*. In his book that bears this phrase as the title, he unpacks at great length the process of learning to capture the lies of the enemy and make them obedient to Christ. As we practice doing this on a regular basis, we learn to interrupt the lies earlier and earlier and turn to Jesus instead of letting those lies shape our thinking. Eventually, the lies lose all power over us as we learn to live on a firm foundation of truth. When it comes to healing the sick, our role as spiritual shepherds is to help others learn to recognize when they are living out of a lie instead of living out of the truth. It looks like saying things to them like:

- "I hear you saying you are worthless, but Psalm 139:14 says you are fearfully and wonderfully made."
- "I hear you saying things that make it seem like you feel like your past defines you, but Paul tells us in 2 Corinthians that we are new creations. Jesus *became* sin, so that we might *become* the very righteousness of God. That past is not who you are anymore."
- "I hear you saying you'll never break free from these chains of sin in your life, but Paul tells us in Romans 8, 'Therefore, dear brothers and sisters, you have *no obligation to do what your sinful nature urges you to do!'* Jesus *wants* you to be free from these sins, and I can help you live into that freedom!"

It might look like helping them develop scripture-based affirmations or truth statements that they can turn to when the lies are ringing loudly in their ears. Things like:

- "In Christ, I am loved even when I feel unlovable."
- "When I feel weak, then I'm actually at my strongest because Jesus' power is made perfect in weakness."
- "I am not worthless; I am a child of the King of all kings."

We have to be very careful not to *weaponize* scripture, but rather share the truth of scripture wrapped in compassion. Every time we help someone recognize that they are living out of a lie and then remind them of the truth, we are helping them take one step closer to understanding and living out of their true identity in Christ. As we shepherd them toward truth, there will likely be a significant *aha* moment for them at some point on their journey, but it doesn't mean the light of truth will always instantaneously replace darkness in their lives.

That's the beauty of light: it always wins. When we flip on a light switch, there isn't an epic battle between the light and the darkness until light eventually vanquishes the darkness and is allowed to shine. Nope! You flip on the switch, and the presence of the light *instantly* overcomes the darkness because darkness is merely the absence of light. By his divine power, God sometimes brings that kind of instantaneous healing to some. For some, truth is found, and instantly, the light of truth roots out any dark lies in their lives. For many others, however, it's a longer journey toward healing and wholeness.

To heal the sick means to remind others that they are not what they feel, not what they fear, and not what they've done. It means reminding them of who they are and whose they are until their identities are firmly rooted in Jesus. This kind of identity work is often less like a light switch and more like a sunrise: It happens a little at a time as the world around us slowly gets brighter and brighter until finally the sun crests the horizon and our bodies are bathed in a full understanding of the light of truth. Except that, in the sunrise of identity work, it ends with *us* becoming the light of Jesus as we learn to shine his light into the world around us.

Some people might barely be on the precipice of starting to see themselves and the world around them by the light of Jesus. Their change in worldview and their sense of identity come little by little as things get brighter and clearer in the light of Jesus. As the process continues, they are eventually bathed in light, and they themselves are set ablaze by that light as it penetrates them. Every step of the way, they shine the light of Christ brighter to others around them as the light shines brighter in their own lives. May we remind ourselves that everyone's sunrise happens at a different pace, and so we would do well to pray for patience as shepherds if their transformation is not happening at the pace we'd prefer. May we pray for patient endurance as we continue to remind them of the truth and offer grace and guidance over time. Healing happens when the lies lose power, and the truth is finally allowed to speak loud enough to shape them to look more like Jesus. Not every breakthrough is dramatic, but all truth moves the sick toward healing because our God is the God of truth.

SELF-CARE AND REFLECTION

Today, I will care for myself and stay connected to God by:

Space for Reflection:

SIX

STRENGTHEN THE WEAK

He gives power to the weak and strength to the powerless...
*But those who trust in the L*ORD *will find new strength.*
ISAIAH 40:29, 31a

AFTER THE SPIRITUAL TRIAGE

I used to be enamored by shows or movies that depict the realities of hospital emergency rooms. To the casual observer, a scene in an ER seems like chaos because there is so much to take in during a moment of intense crisis. In actuality, they are less chaotic than they appear at first glance. The intensity is high, but so is the order of it all. Specifically, emergency rooms are built on an adaptable system of *triage.* Triage is simply the prioritizing of who or what needs attention first. If a person with a minor cut and a person with a gaping wound both come into the ER at the same time, the gaping wound will take priority and get the most energy and attention until that crisis has been mitigated and attention can be turned elsewhere.

In chapter one, I unpacked a little bit of my cycling accident that led to a TBI. A few of the "Polaroids" of memory, which I highlighted in that chapter, are indicative of the triage I was given that day. They first prioritized active external bleeding, moved on to imaging that would rule out any brain bleeds, and ultimately, turned attention to my road rash as the least urgent priority.

We do the same kind of triage as spiritual shepherds. In the darkest of moments, the triage begins with making sure others are safe by asking the hard question surrounding suicidal ideation that we learned in chapter two. Once we are confident in their physical safety, we turn our attention toward being present with them in moments of crisis, as discussed in chapter four. After the initial moment of crisis, our attention is turned toward helping them root their identity in Jesus, as we discussed in the last chapter. This is the process of spiritual triage. We give attention to the needs of those we are walking alongside, starting with the most urgent to least urgent.

But what happens after the spiritual triage? The same thing that happens after emergency room triage: the real work begins. If someone tears a ligament in their knee, the real work begins after knee surgery. The crisis is over, but the journey toward wholeness is just beginning as a plan is made to get back to full strength. They then spend weeks rehabbing and strengthening the knee and the muscles around the knee until they get back to full health. In the same way, after spiritual triage comes the process of *strengthening the weak*.

The truth is, we often forget about this crucial stage of the journey. It can come as such a relief that someone is past the initial crisis that we assume the journey is over once they are no longer in a place of suicidal desperation. After Mendy asked me if I was thinking about killing myself, we quickly found a key piece to my support system: my therapist Brooke. I'm not sure I'd be here without Brooke. She helped me get through my initial crisis of suicidal desperation; she stopped the bleeding. She then helped me gain significant traction in my trauma therapy and, in many ways, gave me the tools that would prepare me (pre-op) for success during my trauma-intensive (surgery).

I'll be forever grateful to Kelley, who was my therapist at the two-week trauma intensive I attended in 2022 at Restoring The Soul. Restoring The Soul is an incredible counseling practice in Lakewood,

Colorado, that focuses on offering one or two-week counseling intensives. Their model of Integrated Clinical Soul Care (ICSC) blends mental health care with spiritual formation and contemplative spirituality in a way that fosters an atmosphere of healing. God used Kelley at Restoring The Soul in some incredible ways to facilitate the wholesale healing that the Holy Spirit brought to me during those two weeks. And when I say wholesale, I mean it. My prayer going into the intensive was that I would gain enough momentum that Brooke (my regular therapist) and I could continue the trauma therapy as I went back to work after my twelve-week leave of absence was over. God showed me that I was not asking big enough. My experience at my Restoring The Soul intensive was so powerful and healing, so complete, that Kelley and I were trying to figure out how to use our time together the last day and a half that I had left. I recognize that's not always how it works. Sometimes, the journey toward healing is a much longer road, but praise God for what he did in rewriting my story that summer.

But after all of that, the strengthening work took center stage. Continued meetings with Brooke were a massive piece of that strengthening work, but many others played a significant role in getting me to a place of strength. I'm grateful I had people in my life who recognized that, after the spiritual triage, the journey toward wholeness and strength was just beginning in earnest. I might have seemed better on the outside after the spiritual triage during my mental health crisis, but I was still fragile within. There is significant temptation to assume the work is done when someone *looks* okay, but the depth of care people need after the emotional storm passes is significant. Thankfully, Bob recognized the depth of care I didn't even know I needed just by looking in my eyes.

WINDOWS TO THE SOUL

A Roman statesman in the first century BC named Cicero wrote, "The face is a picture of the mind, and the eyes are its interpreter."[1] Jesus said it this way: "The eye is the lamp of the body. If your eyes are healthy, your whole body will be full of light."[2] Some combination of these sentiments has often been paraphrased as, "The eyes are the window to the soul." My friend, mentor, and boss, Bob, understands this better than most people I know. Bobby has often told me that he can tell how I'm doing based on my eyes. When I'm *not* okay, he can see the weight, desperation, and exhaustion present in my eyes. When I'm in a good spot, he can tell because the light has come back into my eyes.

More times than I can count, Bobby has checked in with me over the years in such a caring way. When I have admitted that I'm struggling, Bob has often followed up with some version of the statement, "Yeah, I can see it in your eyes." It is powerful to be known so well by a spiritual shepherd. It's one of the reasons I am so passionate about the content of this book; I am who I am today in large part because I've been on the receiving end of so much of what I'm sharing.

I pray that each one of us is given the grace to have a Bobby-like attunement with the Holy Spirit to discern when others are not at their best. That we would take time to look into the souls of others to notice when they are filled with either light or darkness. Then, when we see the weight of darkness in the eyes of others as they walk through a difficult season, I pray we would be able and willing to come alongside them and make ourselves available to be used by God to strengthen the weak. And to be clear: strength doesn't mean solved; it means supported. A tree is only ever as strong as its root system because it is the root system that supports the tree. This is why Paul said in Colossians 2:7, "Let your roots grow down into [Jesus], and let your lives be built on him. Then your faith will grow strong in the truth you were taught, and you will overflow with thankfulness" (NLT).

Strengthening the weak is about helping others grow stronger in their faith. Not just in belief, but in trust, peace, and hope as well. Growing strong in faith is really the process of letting our roots grow deep into Jesus so that, in the midst of storms, he is our support system and strength. It is learning to understand that true strength is not even *our* strength; it's the Holy Spirit in us that gives us strength.

But how do we, practically, grow our roots down into Jesus and invite others to do the same? In two words: spiritual practices.

REARRANGE OUR LIVES AROUND WHAT JESUS SAYS

Jesus spent three years strengthening his disciples. From the moment Jesus called Peter, Andrew, James, and John on the beach in Matthew 4 until the night Jesus was crucified, it was right around three years. Those fishermen left everything behind on the beach to follow Jesus, and follow him they did. They spent virtually every waking moment with Jesus for three straight years, and Jesus strengthened them along the way by both teaching and modeling spiritual practices.

Jesus modeled for and explicitly taught his disciples how to pray. He modeled the importance of silence and solitude to seek God the Father. He taught them how to fast, how to feast, and how to trust God to provide for their needs. Jesus taught them how to serve, how to humble themselves, and how to elevate the lowly. Jesus modeled the importance of knowing God's Word, how to turn the other cheek, and when to speak up for the oppressed.

More might be caught than taught, but the disciples were given opportunities to do both constantly as Jesus taught with his life and his words. As the disciples spent more and more time with Jesus, they were radically transformed to look more like him as they reoriented their entire lives around his teachings by engaging in the spiritual practices he taught and modeled. In the discipleship guide, "Follow," my friend and colleague, Pastor Eric Parks, said, "If Jesus is right—about God, about life, about the soul—then it only makes sense to rearrange your life around what he says is true."[3]

Rearranging our lives around what Jesus taught and modeled is the journey of spiritual formation. It is the process of taking Jesus' yoke upon ourselves and truly becoming disciples of Rabbi Jesus. Formation happens through engagement with spiritual practices that help us create space in our lives and reclaim moments throughout our days to spend more time with Jesus. Ultimately, these practices are what help us rearrange our lives around what he says is true. Again, if more is caught than taught, then the best thing we can do to help strengthen others is to make sure we are living a life that has been radically rearranged around Jesus. This models for others what a deeply rooted life in Jesus looks like, which is appealing. It's compelling. The lives of so many others have inspired me to rearrange more of my life around Jesus. Not because of what they said, but because of how they lived.

We've said it before, but we can't take others further than we've been ourselves. And we can't give what we don't possess. We'll come back to this concept more in chapter nine, but this kind of witness through with-ness is powerful, and it speaks louder than words. And yet, words are also necessary. But how do we equip others with tools that will help them form spiritual rhythms and practices that will help strengthen their faith?

WALK, DON'T POINT

Somewhere along the way, I picked up on the customer service concept "Walk, don't point." If someone asks where the bathroom is at church, I could point across the atrium, and they would probably find it. It's the quickest, easiest response to a simple question. But if I slow down long enough to show them by walking them across the atrium, I would be less likely to miss an opportunity. If they are asking where the bathroom is, it's a pretty good indicator that they are a new atten-der. What better way to help them feel seen, known, and well cared for than by saying, "Let me walk you over there," and asking them a question about themselves on the way over. Walking them over instead of pointing them in the right direction creates opportunity and space for relational proximity.

As we saw earlier, Jesus' whole ministry as he taught his disciples was based on prolonged relational proximity. Jesus was the master of "Walk, don't point." Because of that, I think "Walk, don't point" is much more than a good idea in the realm of customer service. It's also a primary tool for a shepherd. Can you imagine an actual sheepherder trying to get her sheep to go somewhere by pointing in a particular direction? I don't think it would work out all that well. That's why walking is more powerful than pointing as we seek to strengthen the weak. Helping people establish rhythms and practices that will help them strengthen their faith should feel far less like presenting a legalistic list of dos and don'ts and far more like an invitation into something deeper.

Legalistic	Invitational
You really should read your Bible more.	I find that spending time in God's Word helps anchor me in God's truth to start my day. Maybe we could go through the same reading plan together.
Try praying for X number of minutes in the morning.	It's incredible how setting reminders throughout my day to cue me to pray has helped keep me centered on Jesus. Maybe we could set some alarms for the same time to be praying together, even when we aren't around one another.
You don't tithe? You really should start immediately.	It's been amazing to see how practicing generosity has helped me feel less owned by the things I own, and it helps me get outside of myself. What if we came up with a list of things we could give away to show others how valuable they are to us?

Notice how all of the examples are an invitation to come alongside and experience something. Specifically, they are invitations for others to try a practice *with us* in which we've already experienced success. Invitations to join are always more powerful than commands to do something. After all, Jesus started with, "Come and see," long before he commanded the disciples to, "Go and do."

TRIPPING OVER THE TRUTH

I learned early on in student ministry that students don't like to be told what to do. Let's be honest, adults don't either. It took me a while, but after years of getting nowhere fast while telling my students what to do, I dug deep into the recesses of my mind and remembered something I learned in my Psychology of Children and Youth class in college. I even went back and confirmed my suspicions: as students are in a stage of developing a sense of autonomy—the sense of being the author of one's own actions—they are far more likely to make changes when they feel like they are making the decision for themselves to change. Said another way, truth is far more likely to take root in someone's life if we help them trip over that truth rather than shoving it down their throats.

But what does "tripping over the truth" look like? Let me take you back to middle school Tomy, wearing mid-calf Paco shorts, a white tank top, and a bowl cut. If you can't picture it, you're probably better off. Oh, I forgot to mention, I was still in the throes of discovering the importance of personal hygiene. In particular, I had been teased multiple times about the excess earwax that I was particularly adept at producing. The real problem was that I rarely removed said excess earwax. My mom had told me multiple times that I needed to clean out my ears regularly, but to no avail. But then she got smart about it.

I was sitting at a table at a McDonald's in the middle of nowhere, Kansas, on the way to a student mission trip the summer after eighth grade. I was sitting with several friends, as well as one of our adult sponsors Chris. He was out of high school, and I thought he was one of the coolest guys I'd ever met. I don't recall how the conversation started, but I do remember Chris uttering the most unnatural sentence that could have been uttered in that setting: "I find that the best time to clean out my ears is right after I get out of the shower each morning." Even as a naive eighth grader, I could see right through the shenanigans and knew my mom had put him up to it. What were the odds that my mom would keep talking to me about cleaning out my ears over and over again, and then Chris would randomly talk about the same thing? It was obvious—no subtlety whatsoever! But here's the funny thing: IT TOTALLY WORKED! It was one thing for my mom to say it, but if someone as cool as Chris cleaned out his ears that regularly, well then, maybe I should too. As of the writing of this book, I'm an adult male who is about to turn forty, and I still hear Chris' voice in the back of my mind regularly, reminding me to clean out my ears after I get out of the shower. My wife thanks you, Chris.

How in the world did that pathetic ruse work? Because Chris wasn't telling me to do anything, he was simply sharing from his own experience in a way that helped me trip over the truth. Sometimes, it really is that simple. Sometimes, it takes people a lot longer to trip over the truth that we wish they knew. Even if it feels like we've strategically laid the exact right boulder in their path to trip over, they still have to choose for themselves. For every earwax story where I tripped over the truth that someone else was helping me discover, I have three more that took much longer for me to have the desired *aha* moment. If we keep trying our hardest, but it feels like we just can't get through to someone, maybe it's time to do a little digging and figure out which of the four major elements of change is missing.

VISION, INTENTION, MEANS

In the last chapter, we briefly discussed philosopher, theologian, and author Dallas Willard and his seminal book *Renovation of the Heart*. In this book, Willard introduced the acronym VIM, which stands for vision, intention, and means. He argued that if someone is struggling to see change in their life in terms of spiritual formation, they are likely missing one of those three elements. First off, people might be lacking a clear *vision* for what their life could be if they were to surrender that part of themselves to Jesus. Do they understand that the cost of *not* surrendering is greater than the cost of surrendering? Do they have a picture of what a life of freedom, healing, wholeness, and surrender would be like?

Often, this is exactly where the power of testimony shines at its full strength. This is where Lecrae's "scars" conversation comes in. Sure, on some level, people instinctively understand that life will be better on the other side of XYZ, but have they seen it with skin on? This is why Jesus so emphatically tells us to "Let your light shine before others, that they may see your good deeds and glorify your Father in heaven."[4] The best way to help someone see a vision for what a changed life might look like is to live a changed life before them.

If they understand the vision, the next question is that of *intention*. Have they truly chosen to surrender? It's one thing to understand the transformational work Jesus wants to bring, but it's another thing entirely to submit to the work of the Spirit in our lives. Sometimes, our role is to follow the Holy Spirit into a challenging conversation that helps bring others to a place of decision. Remember the support/challenge matrix in chapter one?

My friend Bob once shared a critique he heard about Young Life, the parachurch ministry where he worked for decades. Someone said, "The problem with you Young Life people is that you win the right to be heard by students, and then you win the right to be heard by students, and then, finally, you win the right to be heard by students." The point being that it can be tempting to perpetually earn relational equity that we never cash in on. Have you led gently, been present in moments of crisis, and consistently spoken truth that has helped others find their true identity in Christ? I virtually guarantee that you have built significant relational equity by creating psychological safety in that relationship. If they get the *vision* but still aren't showing *intention* toward growth and surrender, well, I would encourage you to prayerfully ask the Spirit to guide you into a loving yet challenging conversation at the right moment that would invite them to a decision point.

This is where you will have to do your own work of knowing yourself to lead yourself.[5] Neatly threading this needle will be difficult for most of us without great intentionality to grow in this skill. Some of us will tend toward the *rushing* end of the spectrum. Bringing challenge is easy for some of us, so we prematurely bring it before we've earned the right to be heard. This will burn a lot of credibility and may lose the opportunity to continue walking with others. If this is you, proceed with an abundance of caution and lean into prayer before bringing challenge to those who are hurting.

Others, like myself, will lean toward the *dragging our feet* end of the spectrum. We can be so worried about hurting others or disrupting relational harmony that we never get around to bringing challenge. This kind of avoidance isn't being radically *for* them. We have to learn to stop ignoring the Spirit when we feel the nudge to bring challenge that might help them get to a clear decision point.

If they get the *vision,* we see in them the *intention,* but they are still struggling to make any significant progress on their healing journey, then perhaps they are missing the *means.* Do you remember the house metaphor from the Introduction? If someone told me, "You should build a house. A house will provide a place of safety, care, and rich relationships in which you and your family can live." I might hear that and think, "You're right! I *should* build a house!" Well, I've caught the vision of why I should build a house. And I may even have the intention of building said house. But that doesn't mean I know *how* to build a house. Where do I even start? I don't have any land, a blueprint, or any tools. Even if I did have all of those things, that doesn't mean I have the necessary skill to build a house.

This is what people feel when they are lacking *means* in spiritual formation. What are the tools? What are the resources? What is the blueprint for building my life on the firm foundation of Christ? Well, we've hinted at them this entire chapter, but let me introduce you—if you're not already intimately acquainted with—"The Nine" spiritual practices.

THE NINE

In his book *Practicing the Way,* John Mark Comer affectionately refers to his list of nine spiritual practices simply as "The Nine." For Comer, the nine are:

- Sabbath – Setting aside a day for rest and worship
- Solitude – Finding peace amidst noise and busyness
- Prayer – Overcoming distraction to hear God's voice and make our requests known to God
- Fasting – Denying ourselves that we may seek to hear from God
- Scripture – Reading, meditating on, studying, and memorizing God's Word
- Community – Living in a shared spiritual life with others
- Generosity – Practicing giving to others
- Service – Practically meeting the needs of others with Christlike love
- Witness – Sharing the message of the gospel and living it out[6]

Other authors in this space, like Richard J. Foster, would expand this list to twelve or more.[7] To be clear, practicing these disciplines is not a way for us to bring about change by our own power, by simply *doing the right things*. These practices are like gardening. They are tools with which to weed the garden, till the ground, fertilize the soil, and water the seeds so the Holy Spirit can cause fruit to grow in our lives. They are the things we can do to intentionally rearrange our lives around what Jesus says is true as our roots grow down deep into him.

In the summer of 2025, I was gifted with a six-week sabbatical after being the lead student pastor at Plum Creek Church for seven years. That sabbatical was a time to rest, recharge, refocus, and reconnect with my family. More importantly, it was an opportunity to intentionally seek God for the next season of my life and ministry. On night one of my sabbatical, I heard God clearly asking me, "Would you say more of your life is pointed toward spiritual formation or instant gratification?" *Oof!* What a way to start a sabbatical.

At first, I thought, "Well, of *course*, my life is pointed toward spiritual formation. I read my Bible. I pray. I constantly read books about personal growth and theology." But then I had this thought, "Which one would my phone screen-time report say I prioritize?" Again, *oof!* I started to realize how many opportunities throughout my days, weeks, months, and years that I relinquish to instant gratification—quick hits of dopamine from a device or screen—when I could be investing those moments in spiritual formation. Five minutes here, an hour there, a day of binge-watching now and again starts to add up to a pretty significant amount of time throughout the year.

What if, instead of pulling out my phone to check sports scores, I spent five minutes reciting memory verses for the week to re-center myself in Jesus? What if, instead of binging a podcast every time I'm alone in the car, I used it as a chance to sit in silence so God could quiet my mind and bring me peace? What if, instead of having the TV on in the background while I fold laundry every Friday, I spent time praying over my family as I fold their clothes? Notice how none of these things requires me to *create* time or space in my week. Instead, these are ways that I've been trying to intentionally *reclaim* opportunities to go about my day, keeping Jesus at the center rather than filling those moments with noise.

"The Nine" are the means by which we can focus more of our lives on being formed by Jesus rather than being formed by influencers, celebrities, and the world at large. At their worst, "The Nine" can be weaponized by modern-day Pharisees for a framework of legalism. At their best, however, practicing them is an invitation into a deeper, richer life that is centered on Jesus and the work of the Holy Spirit in our lives. They are tried and true ways of creating space in our lives for the fruit of the Spirit to grow and flourish. And who among us couldn't use more love, joy, peace, patience, kindness, goodness, faithfulness, gentleness, and self-control? Who among us couldn't stand to be strengthened in our faith? As spiritual shepherds, the life that these practices produce is the very life we should be inviting others into. That invitation and the practical coaching that accompanies it are the very process of strengthening the weak.

THE BLOCK OF ICE

The small group leaders in our ministry have likely grown weary of hearing about the block of ice. In his book, *Atomic Habits*, author James Clear uses the following illustration.

Imagine we are sitting in a room that is 20°F, and there is a massive block of ice in the center of the room. What would happen to the block of ice if we raised the temperature of that room by 1°? Well, nothing, because the freezing point of water is 32°F. But what if we raised it by another degree, and another, and another? Still, nothing would happen to that block of ice. But if we kept going and eventually got the temperature of the room to 32° or 33°, well, something interesting would start happening. We would see a little bit of sweat on the block of ice. If we kept raising the temperature of the room 1° at a time until we hit 70°, and left it long enough, well, it wouldn't matter how big the block of ice was. It would eventually be a puddle.

As spiritual shepherds, we can't control the outcomes; that is the job of the Holy Spirit. What we *can* control is showing up consistently, moment after moment, day after day, week after week, to help put in that 1° difference until we finally see glimmers of the change we've been fervently praying for all along. When we finally see a little bit of sweat forming on the ice in the lives of those we are shepherding, it is wildly exciting! There will be moments of breakthrough. They will have finally tripped over the truth, caught the vision, made the choice, and asked for help with the means. Those will be moments of great joy and celebration, not only in our hearts, but in heaven as well.

But what if we have been putting in the effort for so long, and we're still not seeing the results we want? Friends, I know how disheartening that can be. I have felt the pain, and I feel the pain with you. But please, don't give up. Again, we are not in charge of the outcomes. The only thing we can control is showing up consistently to put in that 1° difference until the Holy Spirit brings about the change we are praying for. Do not be discouraged; you might be sitting at 30°, only a couple of degrees away from a significant breakthrough. Just because we aren't seeing the results we want to see, it doesn't mean the atmosphere in their life isn't changing in a way that will eventually bring about those results in God's timing. Paul reminded us of this.

> So let's not get tired of doing what is good. At just the right time we will reap a harvest of blessing if we don't give up."
> GALATIANS 6:9, NLT

Keep inviting them into the presence of Jesus through shared spiritual practices. Keep speaking truth louder than the enemy is speaking lies. Keep going to God on their behalf in intercessory prayer, trusting that the Lord of the harvest loves them more than we ever could.

PATIENT ENDURANCE

You might have noticed that earlier I said there were potentially four elements of change that might be missing, but I then proceeded to unpack only three of them: Dallas Willard's *vision*, *intention*, and *means*. If you have tendencies toward obsessive-compulsive behaviors, I'm very sorry for the last few pages of intense internal tension that I created within you. I do believe the silent partner of Willard's VIM model is a phrase given to us by the Apostle Peter: patient endurance. This phrase is like the protagonist d'Artagnan to Porthos, Athos, and Aramis in Alexandre Dumas' *Three Musketeers*. Though the story is named for the moniker of Athos, Porthos, and Aramis collectively, it is d'Artagnan who joins them, binds them together, and, most importantly, embodies the posture that allows their shared mission to endure. In the same way, patient endurance does not replace vision, intention, or means; it animates them. It is the lived perseverance that carries transformation forward when progress feels slow, resistance is real, and formation takes longer than we hoped. Without patient endurance, the VIM model remains conceptually sound but practically fragile. With it, change becomes sustainable.

In view of all this, make every effort to respond to God's promises. Supplement your faith with a generous provision of moral excellence, and moral excellence with knowledge, and knowledge with self-control, and self-control with patient endurance, and patient endurance with godliness, and godliness with brotherly affection, and brotherly affection with love for everyone.

2 PETER 1:5-7, NLT

I love the progression Peter gives us here. He tells us that responding to God's promises starts with supplementing our faith—not with a small dose, not with a single serving, but with a *generous provision* of moral excellence. If I'm honest with myself, too often, I settle for a teaspoon of moral good-enough-ness, but that's neither here nor there. The point I see Peter making is that we should start by wholeheartedly pursuing what we know to be morally good. We should start by committing ourselves to doing what we intrinsically know to be right and doing those things with excellence.

From there, we add knowledge so we can grow beyond our understanding of what is right and wrong. And it's safe to assume Peter would encourage us to ensure the knowledge we add is rooted in Christ. Knowledge surrounding what Jesus said was true about God, life, and the soul. As we add that knowledge—once we know what Jesus said—Peter said we have to practice self-control as we strive to rearrange our lives around what Jesus said is true. Doing so will help us live out of Jesus' ethic and worldview—a way of life centered around love in the kingdom of God. Loving God, loving others, even loving our enemies. But before we get there—before we grow in godliness—what will very likely be required is *patient endurance*. Habits simply are not formed in an instant.

As shepherds seeking to strengthen the weak, perhaps our best expenditure of energy would be in cheering on and encouraging those we shepherd. Inevitably, they will try to move toward rooting themselves in Jesus. They will try engaging in practices that will allow the Holy Spirit to shape them to look more like Jesus. And they will likely even get a small taste of success; they will feel the difference it makes to prioritize spiritual formation over instant gratification. But then, the enemy will find a way to discourage them. In those moments, remind them of the ice block. Encourage them that they might only be one or two degrees away from seeing a significant breakthrough. Remind them that strength is built over time, and it begins with abiding, not achieving. Help them keep going because it is the patient endurance that will bring about godliness, which is what develops true and lasting strength in their faith.

THE "E" WORD

"What is all the fuss about?" When I was in kindergarten, I had an argument with my sister Cynthia in the kitchen of our family home. She is ten years older than I am, so I'm certain I was doing something to annoy her in a way that only little brothers are capable of doing. Our mom came into the kitchen to discover the source of *the fuss*, and I proceeded to tell her, "Cynthia called me the E word!" I remember the look of confusion on my mom's face as she inquired as to the meaning of the E word. We had just moved to Colorado a few months earlier, after growing up most of my life in West Texas, so I hope you can hear and feel how thick my five-year-old southern accent was as I said, "EEE-DIOT!"

The E word would pop up again years later when my daughter Laney was turning one. She was on the verge of taking her first steps, and, as fate would have it, she took those first steps in the presence of our church small group friends in Lakeland, Florida—the group that was affectionately known as the Aunties and Unclers. Everyone seemed to notice all at once that Laney had let go of her walker and was working up the courage to take her first unassisted steps.

We all looked on with bated breath as Laney went *step...step... wobble...step...fall.* And the moment she fell, everyone erupted with loud boos and hissing! I ran over and yelled in Laney's face, "You eee-diot! Can't you even take three steps without falling?"

Okay, before you rightfully call child-protective services on me, let me just say, "OF COURSE THAT'S NOT WHAT HAPPENED!" Laney went *step...step...wobble...step...fall,* and the moment she fell, everyone erupted with whoops, excited clapping, and exuberant cheers of support! Why? Because we weren't disappointed that she fell, we were proud of her for taking the steps.

The journey of strengthening the weak will be just like helping a toddler learn how to walk. They will be wobbly and scared at first. The likelihood that they will fall now and again is high because relapses are often part of the journey toward recovery. Grief and healing aren't linear, and spiritual formation isn't a straight line up and to the right. The question very likely isn't, "Will they fall?" The question is, "Will someone be there to help them up *when* they fall?" When my daughter Laney fell over and over again as she was learning to walk, I was there every single time to pick her up, encourage her, and tell her to keep trying.

If, even I, as a flawed human father, had this kind of attitude toward my children as they learned to walk, how much more will our heavenly Father be there to say, "Get up! You can do this! I believe in you! Just keep your eyes on me and keep taking more and more steps in between falls as you learn to depend on the holy spirit to sustain you!" As spiritual shepherds, be the hands and feet of Jesus, waiting to pick them up, encourage them, and help them fix their eyes on their heavenly Father as they are strengthened by the Holy Spirit.

As of the writing of this book, Laney is now eleven years old. If she *still* couldn't take more than three or four steps in between falls, well, it would be an indication that something was wrong. An eleven-year-old who constantly wobbles and falls every few steps is developmentally inappropriate, and, as her father, it would be up to me to help her figure out what was causing it. I might not be able to figure it out on my own, but I could help her find the expert who could. Similarly, if those we are shepherding can't seem to develop and grow stronger in their faith, it would be spiritual malpractice to ignore it.

God doesn't flinch when his children fall; he leans in. And so must we. Strengthening the weak means celebrating courage, steadying trembling legs, and guiding them back to the Father's steadying voice as they learn to take more and more steps in between falls. But it also means loving them enough to notice when their legs just won't hold them up and helping them find someone who can help identify why—like a Christian counselor (more on that in chapter eight). Shepherds don't look away; they look deeper. Because strengthening the weak isn't just about preventing falls, it's about helping our sheep form a life that keeps rising.

SELF-CARE AND REFLECTION

Today, I will care for myself and stay connected to God by:

Space for Reflection:

SEVEN

YOUR GOOD SHEPHERD

I am the good shepherd. The good shepherd lays down his life for the sheep.
JOHN 10:11, ESV

WHAT IF I'M NOT ENOUGH?

"This is a stupid activity! I would be embarrassed to be good at it!" There is a scene in the American version of *The Office*—a television show about everyday life at a paper company—where Dwight tries slacklining for the first time. If you've never seen it, slacklining is an activity where someone attempts to walk across a flat strap tied between two anchor points—like a tightrope, but wider and usually with more bounce. After a montage of Dwight failing miserably several times in a row, he stands up, turns to his coworkers, and with a bloody lip, delivers the line above. The scene is intended to be played for laughs, but there was something that hit a little too close to home the first time I watched it.

There have been long stretches of my life when I refused to give anything my full effort. At times, this lackadaisical attitude came from insufficient energy as I walked through seasons of depression. At other times, it was full-blown laziness. Every time I phoned it in, I

113

tried to act like the lack of effort was because trying simply wasn't cool. Years ago, a friend and coworker tried to teach me a new game to play with students in order to pass some idle time together. When I realized very quickly that I wasn't going to excel at the game, I stopped trying altogether, prompting my friend to shout in frustration, "There isn't a competitive bone in your body, is there?" This anecdote is a microcosm of my attitude for long periods of time, where it was easier and safer to act like I didn't care enough to try. In reality, at the core of each of those moments or seasons of apathy was a fear of failure. Even if I wasn't aware of it at the time, I can look back and see that I was terrified of trying my best and coming up short. I was terrified of finding the answer to the question, "What if I'm not enough?"

If you've made it this far in the book, there's a decent chance you're feeling the weight of this call to care for and shepherd others and all that comes with it. Depending on your history and wiring, this weight might feel overwhelming or even unbearable. If you have found yourself asking, "What if I try to help others and I'm not enough?", let me ease your burden: you are NOT enough, but Christ *in* you is more than enough. Paul told us as much in 2 Corinthians 12:9-10.

> But he said to me, "My grace is sufficient for you, for my power is made perfect in weakness." Therefore I will boast all the more gladly about my weaknesses, so that Christ's power may rest on me. That is why, for Christ's sake, I delight in weaknesses, in insults, in hardships, in persecutions, in difficulties. For when I am weak, then I am strong.

Friends, the question is not, "Can *you* heal them?" The question is, "Can you show up as the hands and feet of the one who *can* heal them?" Remember, you are simply participating in a divine collaboration. You are not the Good Shepherd—that should feel like a relief—but the Good Shepherd is with you. The Good Shepherd goes before you. The Good Shepherd has sent you an advocate. He promised this in John 14:26-27.

> But the Advocate, the Holy Spirit, whom the Father will send in my name, will teach you all things and will remind you of everything I have said to you. Peace I leave with you; my peace I give you. I do not give to you as the world gives. Do not let your hearts be troubled and do not be afraid.

We can take heart knowing the Good Shepherd got it right where the shepherds of Israel got it wrong. Jesus was, in the flesh, the redemptive reversal of the indictment against the spiritual shepherds of Israel in Ezekiel 34:4. He showed us how to live that redemptive reversal, and he contrasted each point with his life and his words.

The weak you have not strengthened.	Luke 22 – I've prayed for you . . . strengthen your brothers.
The sick you have not healed.	Mark 5 – Daughter, your faith has made you well.
The injured you have not bound up.	John 11 – Jesus weeps with Mary before raising Lazarus.
The strays you have not rounded up.	John 21 – Jesus restores Peter on the beach.
The lost you have not sought.	Luke 19 – The Son of Man came to seek and save the lost.
With force and harshness, you have ruled them.	Matthew 11 – I am gentle and humble in heart.

Jesus is the fulfillment of what bad shepherds failed to do and the example for those who want to shepherd well. In John 10, he told us that he knows his sheep by name. He lays down his life for them. He goes before them. Friends, *we* are the sheep he goes before. Trust that, in every shepherding conversation, in every moment of crisis, in every life-or-death situation, the Good Shepherd goes before us as we step out to shepherd others, and the Holy Spirit is with us always. Not only that, but Jesus wants to do for us what we are called to do for others.

PSALM 23

If you want to know how Jesus longs to shepherd us as we let him shepherd others through us, sit with Psalm 23 for a while. Meditate on it slowly. Memorize it. Internalize it. Read it until it reads you.

> The Lord is my shepherd, I lack nothing. He makes me lie down in green pastures, he leads me beside quiet waters, he refreshes my soul. He guides me along the right paths for his name's sake.
>
> Even though I walk through the darkest valley, I will fear no evil, for you are with me; your rod and your staff, they comfort me. You prepare a table before me in the presence of my enemies. You anoint my head with oil; my cup overflows. Surely your goodness and love will follow me all the days of my life, and I will dwell in the house of the Lord forever.

Go back and read it again. Now, read it again. When you feel like you've read it enough, read it a few more times. Come back when you're ready. How does it feel knowing the Good Shepherd so badly wants to shepherd you? The framework here is incredible.

Vs 1 – I lack nothing.	He will provide for my every need because he is all that I need.
Vs 2 – He makes me lie down.	He gives me rest if only I will slow down and let Him.
Vs 2 – He leads me beside quiet waters.	He will calm my heart and mind if I meet him in stillness and solitude.
Vs 3 – He refreshes my soul.	He provides energy, life, and healing.
Vs 3 – He guides me.	He gives me direction and helps me show up in ways that are helpful to others.
Vs 4 – You are with me.	I am never alone.
Vs 4 – Your rod and staff comfort me.	I am safe, seen, and soothed.
Vs 5 – You prepare a table for me in the presence of my enemies.	He provides provision and honors me even before those who set themselves against me.
Vs 5 – You anoint my head with oil.	I am chosen, empowered, and commissioned to do his work of shepherding others.
Vs 6 – Goodness and love will follow me.	He goes both before and behind me. I am surrounded by his presence.
Vs 6 – I will dwell.	In both the now and in what is to come, he is my home. In his presence is where I truly belong.

Friends, it's powerful. What more could we ask for? How could we not step confidently into our roles as spiritual shepherds, knowing we are shepherded so well? If it still feels scary, you're not alone. Taking a bold step of faith is always scary. It's meant to be scary. That trepidation reminds us that something is on the line. In those moments, follow David's cue and stop talking *about* God and start crying out *to* God. Go back and read it one more time.

Did you notice the shift? In the darkest moment, David moved from proclaiming truths *about* God to crying out *to God.* Proclaiming and reminding ourselves of truths about God are important practices. They remind us of who we are because of whose we are. They remind us of where our true identity lies and from where our power comes. And yet, they are no substitute for crying out to God himself in times of trouble.

If we hope to help others experience the powerful healing of God, we first have to experience it. If we want to lead them to cry out to the Good Shepherd for help and strength, we first have to make a habit of crying out to the Good Shepherd for help and strength. If we want them to fully anchor their identities in Christ, their redeemer, we must first fully anchor our identity in Christ, our redeemer. Remember, Jesus wants to do for us what he is calling us to do for others, and we cannot show up as wounded healers unless we allow him to begin healing us first. We cannot offer what we have not first received. So, pause for a few minutes and ask the Holy Spirit to empower and embolden you as a shepherd. Cry out to God the Father, asking him to guard and guide you. Ask him to refresh your soul. Ask him to take the weights you carry off your shoulders and to replace them with a blessing of peace, comfort, and joy. Ask him to give you a bold willingness to step into the pain with others as his hands and feet. Sit with the Good Shepherd for a while.

THE SHEPHERD-KING

King David is sometimes referred to as the shepherd-king. Before Jesus was ever called the Good Shepherd, Israel had already seen what that title could mean. King David—the man after God's own heart—was first a shepherd before he ever wore a crown. He learned to lead not from a throne, but from the fields; not by commanding armies, but by guiding sheep through wild terrain. His rise from obscurity to kingship was so improbable, so unexpected, that it shaped Israel's imagination of what godly leadership could look like—not status-driven but servant-hearted. It's no accident that God chose David's lineage to bring forth the Messiah. Jesus, like David, would be a king —but unlike any the world expected.

Israel expected the coming Messiah to be a warrior-king, riding on a white horse to free them from the perpetual oppression of God's people. From Egypt to Assyria, Babylon, Persia, Greece, and Rome, the Israelites fell under the rule of dictator after dictator, and the coming Messiah would put an end to their oppression once and for all by establishing God's rule on earth, or so they thought. Jesus did, indeed, come to establish the kingdom of God, but not in the way they imagined. Rather than finally putting God's people at the top of the food chain, Jesus firmly established that their proper place was at the bottom.

Theologian N.T. Wright often talks about the scandal of the gospel being the claim that God is king *now*. And yet, we live in the tension of the now and not yet. His kingdom is here, and yet it's also coming. His reign is now, and yet it's also to come. The beauty is that God chooses to usher in his kingdom through us bit by bit, piece by piece, moment by moment until—as we said in the Introduction—one day the eastern sky will tear open, and God will arrive to reign forever as King.

Shepherding others through seasons of pain and mental health struggle is one of the clearest ways we can make ourselves available to be used by God to make his kingdom come to earth as it is in heaven. But if we are to be reflections of our coming King, we have to remind ourselves of how things operate in his kingdom. Jesus is often thought of as the second Adam, having come to recast a vision for what it looks like to be fully human under God's rule. So, too, he becomes the true Shepherd-King, not by echoing the power structures of David or Caesar, but by showing what it looks like when divine kingship takes on flesh and kneels to serve. He shows us what it looks like in his kingdom to shepherd others with care and compassion. Jesus turns the world's understanding of power on its head by inaugurating a kingdom where the last are first, the meek are elevated, and greatness is found in service.

In Wright's words, "Jesus was not proclaiming a kingdom that would advance through force of arms but through the force of self-giving love."[1] Just as Jesus redefined humanity by becoming the new Adam, He redefined kingship by becoming the true Shepherd-King, not by ascending to a throne, but by washing feet. Not by crushing enemies, but by carrying a cross. Not by a show of force, but by a show of humility.

David taught us what a shepherd-king could look like, but Jesus fulfilled that vision completely. And now, he invites us to lead in the same way, not by climbing ladders, but by picking up towels. Not by guarding thrones, but by opening doors to healing. Not by demanding to be followed, but by inviting others into a new way of life—gently, patiently, sacrificially—as the Good Shepherd always does.

CITIZENS OF THE SHEPHERD'S KINGDOM

Friends, all of this matters because we are called to live as citizens of the Shepherd's kingdom in the here and now. From the life that our Good Shepherd modeled—the life we are invited to live as well—we can see that the sick and broken are welcomed and even prioritized. Jesus himself said, "Healthy people don't need a doctor—sick people do. I have come to call not those who think they are righteous, but those who know they are sinners."[2] As citizens of the Shepherd's kingdom, may we, too, prioritize the sick and broken. May we seek the lost, round up the strays, bind up the injured, heal the sick, and strengthen the weak as we gently lead them to the throne of the Shepherd-King.

In the Shepherd's kingdom, we see that healing is not transactional; it's relational. Jesus never demanded payment or favors from those he healed. If ever he gave them instructions after he healed them, it was to keep quiet, for it wasn't time for his fame to spread. Or his instructions were more of an invitation into a new way of life, like telling the woman caught in adultery to go and leave her life of sin, because her identity was no longer that of a sinner. Never was healing in any way transactional with Jesus. Instead, he led and healed in a relational way. May we, too, shepherd others relationally rather than transactionally. If we show up to shepherd others with the expectation or hope that we will get something in return, then we are showing up with the wrong motives.

And in the Shepherd's kingdom, shepherding is not hierarchical; it's incarnational—God *with* us and God *through* us. The incarnation of Jesus points to the power of God stepping down from his throne in order to come to the very earth he created, that we may see love in the flesh. Philosopher and theologian Søren Kierkegaard said it this way, "In matters of love, one cannot send a proxy; in matters of love, the king himself must go." And so, Jesus himself came to be Immanuel, God with us, that he may show us God's love in the flesh. We, too, are to shepherd in an incarnational way. As we discussed in chapter one, to declare our witness as with-ness. May we create spaces for the hurting as pastures for healing. And in those pastures, may we once more be reminded that we carry with us the presence of the Holy Spirit, which means we ourselves are hope incarnate.

VISION STATEMENT

As a staff at my church, we were encouraged to write a vision statement for our lives—a simple, one-sentence statement that will remind us of who God is shaping us to be. Remember Willard's VIM model, and you'll get the vision behind the vision. We were challenged that, if we are going to actively engage in spiritual formation, we have to start with a clear picture of what we are being formed into.

At a high level, as followers of Jesus, every one of us is being formed more into his likeness. Paul told us this in 2 Corinthians 3:18.

> So all of us who have had that veil removed can see and reflect the glory of the Lord. And the Lord—who is the Spirit—makes us more and more like him as we are changed into his glorious image (NLT).

So, really, that's the answer for all of us: our vision is being shaped to look more like Jesus as the Holy Spirit grows his fruit in our lives. But where and how does this become uniquely *your* vision? What is

God's specific vision for *your* life? Dallas Willard challenged us to think about it in these terms: How would Jesus live his life if he were you? For me, that question becomes, "How would Jesus live his life if he were an almost forty-year-old student pastor in Colorado in 2025 as the father of two children and the husband of Mendy?" For you, maybe it's, "How would Jesus live his life if he were a single mom of three kids working two jobs just to get by?" Or, "How would Jesus live his life if he were a small business owner or tattoo artist or [fill in the blank]?"

The vision statement is meant to be less about a vision for how or when you'll spend time with Jesus and more about *what would happen* if you prioritized time with him. How would you change? What would you become? How would you show up in the different spaces in your life? Here's mine:

> I will follow Jesus so closely that his dust marks my life, bearing the Spirit's fruits, as I become a force for *liberation,* and I *shepherd* my family and my flock and leave a generational *legacy of faith* as God the Father builds his kingdom through me.

A little bit of *how*—time with Jesus, fruits of the Spirit—and a lot of what it will lead to—liberation, shepherding, and a legacy of faith. I try to read this vision statement once a week. Keeping the vision at the forefront of my mind helps me stay focused on who I'm becoming in Christ by the grace and power of the Holy Spirit. Set aside some time to prayerfully consider where your life is heading by asking the Spirit to reveal who you are to become. When you know who you are becoming, it opens the door for stepping into shepherding situations with great confidence because you know you're being sent by the Good Shepherd, not because the Good Shepherd is desperate and will send anyone, but because a shepherd is who he's shaping you to be.

I encourage you to write your own vision statement. Let it inspire you to keep going when you feel weak. Let it be a reason to get up when you fall. Let it draw you closer to the good shepherd as you shepherd others.

OBEDIENCE, NOT OUTCOMES

My friend Lane is becoming like Jesus. I see it happening before my very eyes. He's learning to surrender. He's seeking to make choices that will honor God and others. He's becoming more and more attuned to the Holy Spirit. So much so that he called me recently while he was at the airport, saying, "Pastor Tomy, this lady is eating her breakfast at the airport, and I feel like I should go pray for her. What do I do?" Now, Lane is a gregarious guy, but he doesn't make a habit of walking up to strangers at the airport and striking up a conversation out of nowhere, so I knew this wasn't a fluke moment. Lane was being prompted by the Holy Spirit.

"Well, Lane, I think you should go offer to pray for her," I responded simply. I coached him a bit on how to approach her and then told him to call me back after the moment was over. Maybe two minutes later, he called me back and said, "Well, I'm betting based on how quickly I called you back that you can guess what happened. She said no." I could hear the disappointment in his voice, so I made sure to go above and beyond in encouraging him and telling him how proud I was of him for being obedient.

Friends, I want to tell you the same thing I told my friend Lane: your responsibility lies in obedience, not outcomes. The outcomes simply are not yours to own—the negative outcomes *or* the positive outcomes. Again, the healing will only be done by the Good Shepherd, who is also known by another name: Great Physician. Disavow yourself early and often of a need to carry the weight of outcomes. Your weight to carry is the weight of obedience.

Who knows what ripple effects Lane's offer to pray for a random lady in an airport might have in her life at some point down the line? Maybe all she needed to know was that there are people out there who care enough to offer to pray for her. Maybe it wasn't even about her. Maybe some other random bystanders saw Lane's actions and heard his words and were emboldened in their faith. Like Abraham and Isaac on the altar, maybe all God needed to see was Lane's obedience in something small to know he was ready to handle the weight of obedience in something bigger down the road.

In the same way, may you be emboldened to simply respond in obedience. May you, too, follow the promptings of the Holy Spirit deep within you and make yourself available. Your obedience might change someone's life, but I am confident it will change *yours*. Pray fervently for positive outcomes with those you are shepherding, but know that those outcomes are not yours to own. You don't have to carry the weight of every sheep. That's not your job. Your calling is to reflect the heart of the Good Shepherd by strengthening the weak, healing the sick, binding up the injured, rounding up the strays, seeking the lost, and leading gently. When we do these things, we point back (always back) to the one who laid down his life for every single one of us. *He* is the Good Shepherd. And he is very, *very* good.

SELF-CARE AND REFLECTION

Today, I will care for myself and stay connected to God by:

Space for Reflection:

EIGHT

A TALE OF REDEMPTION

Go out quickly to the streets and lanes of the city,
and bring in the poor and crippled and blind and lame.
LUKE 14:21, ESV

WHAT LIES AHEAD

F riends, thank you dearly for making it this far. I am beyond
grateful for your willingness to soak up all you can to feel
equipped to shepherd the lost, hurting, and spiritually dry to the feet
of Jesus. I believe you are actively participating in the Holy Spirit's
work of ushering in the kingdom of the Shepherd King. Keep going.
Keep showing up. Keep making a difference.

To all of my friends and readers who are lay leaders—those not in
vocational ministry in some form or fashion—this book has been
written for you. I hope and pray it has prepared you to lean in for
those in your life who are hurting. I have a favor to ask as we begin
this leg of our journey together: please give a copy of this book to a
pastor or elder at your church. If they seem reticent to read it, ask
them to at least take a look at this chapter. Much of what will be
discussed in it will be a call for the vocational shepherds among us to

work hard to ensure our churches and ministries are safe havens for people struggling with their mental health. It will be a plea to make sure those in places of suicidal desperation feel safe to share that burden with others and seek help from their shepherds rather than hiding in plain sight in shame. From your seat, perhaps you can influence those in leadership to take the necessary steps toward emotional and psychological safety for your fellow congregants and friends.

To my pastor friends, I want to share a true story that outlines a multi-year effort to destigmatize mental health and invite our students to seek help rather than struggle alone. My prayer is that at least some part of this story will resonate with you and, perhaps, equip you in some small way to do the same. What lies ahead is one ministry's effort to combat a slew of troubling statistics about death by suicide among teenagers, but the steps we have taken would apply to people of all ages.

Holy Spirit, open our hearts to your movement. Make us attentive and responsive to your promptings. Guide us as we shepherd your flocks.
Amen.

THE JOURNEY TOWARD PSYCHOLOGICAL SAFETY

I moved to my current church as the lead student pastor in August 2018. Given that this new church was only about thirty minutes north of my previous church, I felt like I had a head start in knowing the cultural norms of the surrounding community. I already mentioned in the Introduction that my journey of mental health education began a year prior, when Colorado Springs experienced a cluster of ten students who died by suicide in a two-week period. That led to my first exposure to some of the resources available as I attended a Youth Mental Health First Aid (YMHFA) course (Mental Health First Aid is to mental health as CPR is to the body). It is aimed at helping first aiders recognize signs of a mental health crisis and connect them to resources. I learned so much in attending that training and, because of it, the importance of fostering open dialogue within our faith communities was already deeply planted in my mind as I took on the lead student pastor role at Plum Creek Church in Castle Rock.

That first year or so was a chance to get my bearings and get to know the team, our families, and the surrounding community. In the fall of 2019, a year into my tenure at Plum Creek, we had an outreach event for our high school students. Prayerfully, we decided it would be a good opportunity to teach on a subject that would open the door to a conversation surrounding mental health. I remember the students being overly squirmy during my message as I started talking about anxiety, depression, and death by suicide. We felt the weight in the room and could sense the discomfort for our students.

At the end of the service, with all heads bowed and eyes closed, we invited students to raise their hands if they wanted prayer for mental health struggles. It felt like a fairly low-risk ask, and yet the response was minimal. We didn't get an exact count, but our team agreed it was somewhere around ten students out of well over one hundred in attendance. Not only did it *feel* like a drastic under-representation of students experiencing some level of struggle with their mental health, but we knew from individual conversations with students, parents, and small group leaders that the number should have been much higher.

Through multiple conversations as a team, we began to realize the problem was a problem of stigma and psychological safety. That event helped us realize that students felt unsafe to talk about their mental health. We heard anecdotal stories from students that their parents were telling them to keep quiet about being in counseling or therapy. We expressly had parents tell us their students were worried that others might find out what they were going through. Now, to be clear, it is the right of each individual to decide when, how, and even *if* they want to talk about their mental health journey. Our aim was not to create a culture where students felt *pressured* to talk about their mental health struggles, but to create a culture where students felt safe to ask for help with their mental health struggles.

The first thing we did was invite my friend David to train our staff and key contributors, along with a handful of others in our community, in YMHFA. Just like it did for me, giving our team some tools increased their confidence to know how to show up well. It gave us shared language and knowledge to be able to recognize signs that our students might be experiencing a mental health crisis. We started looking for opportunities to talk about mental health in conversations, even from the platform—not necessarily sermons or series expressly about mental health, but being attuned enough to the Holy Spirit to know when we could make a mention of mental health as it fit naturally.

I became an advocate for talking about mental health from the platform to our adult congregation as well. It wasn't enough to destigmatize the conversation with students if we weren't also destigmatizing it with their parents. We were able to host a parent workshop with a panel of mental health experts, thanks to the help of our friends Steve and Veronica Johnson of Envision Counseling Clinic, and answer questions from parents. We also went on a campaign to make sure we were using appropriate language surrounding mental health that would decrease stigma and increase safety. I've done my best to model that kind of language throughout this book.

I can't really say we were seeing immense progress. It's hard to know after all. What we were certain of was that our staff and key contributors/small group leaders felt more equipped and confident in their ability to help. We were actively engaged and taking steps on the journey toward psychological safety and destigmatizing the need to ask for help with mental health struggles. We were anecdotally having more conversations with parents about their concern for the mental health of their students. Through it all, we created more opportunities to encourage the use of mental, emotional, and spiritual tools to pursue health. Then, the world shut down.

THE STORM BEFORE THE CALM BEFORE THE STORM

To any of my pastor friends who were in vocational ministry before COVID and are still in vocational ministry today, God bless you. COVID was impossible as a leader in the church, and it took a significant toll on everyone—pastors, leaders, parents, and students. The Enneagram 7s (enthusiasts) and other extroverts among us were crumbling under the forced isolation. The Enneagram 8s (challengers) had their blood just below a constant boil from being told what they could and could not do. The 6s (loyalists) were feeling like every deepest, darkest fear was coming to life, and the lack of safety wreaked havoc. The 5s (investigators) and other extreme introverts, well, they were doing okay.

As an Enneagram 9 (peacemaker), the worst part of COVID was that no matter what decision we made, people were angry. If we followed the government guidelines or mandates, people were angry. If we *didn't* follow the government guidelines or mandates, people were angry. If I wasn't fired up and showing emotion to the level that they thought I *should* be, people were angry. If I didn't join with political rhetoric, people were angry. If I used the *wrong* language, people were angry. If I used the *right* language, people were angry.

I choose to believe that, more often than not, people's anger in that season wasn't intended to be aimed directly at me. It's just that anger, turmoil, and frustration were constantly bubbling beneath the surface for so many during that season that it only took the tiniest pinprick for all of that pressure to explode as people saw an opportunity to unleash it. Remember, "Unexpressed emotions will never die. They are buried alive and will come forth later in uglier ways."

I'm sure you can imagine how hard that would be for someone whose core motivation in life is peace in relationships. I was not doing okay, but neither was anyone else. We all experienced collective trauma during COVID, and, for many people, it was like gas on the fire of any underlying mental health concern that already existed. The number of mental health crises exploded during and after 2020 and early 2021. We were beyond grateful that, by God's providence, we were ahead of the game in our quest to create a safe space for students to seek help with their mental health.

As we began meeting again in person, we sought to continue providing resources, normalizing the conversation, and equipping our leaders more and more. We had individual conversations as a means of checking in on students. We continued a coordinated effort that we had begun during the lockdown to reach out to every student in our system to see how they were doing. We continued talking about it from the platform. We intentionally used specific words like depression, anxiety, and suicide from the platform because not using the words can unintentionally communicate to our people that we don't want to be talking about it.

As a church, we created resource cards that we placed in every bathroom of the church, which provided a lengthy list of mental health resources so people could get help even if they didn't feel comfortable talking to us about their journey. It felt like honesty and vulnerability were increasing. We had more and more small group leaders coming to us to ask for advice on how to come alongside their students on their mental health journey, which we took as a sign that students were feeling more and more comfortable asking for help, support, and encouragement.

Then, in September 2021, we had another outreach event for our high school students. Somehow, we had even more students at this one than our event in 2019, despite a spike in inconsistent attendance within our wider church body due to COVID. We invited a guest communicator named Eric Samuel Timm. Eric is a *wildly* gifted communicator as well as an artist, and he is so engaging because he combines both in his sermons. Eric will paint a picture within a few minutes during the worship segment before his teachings, and then it will serve as a visual representation of the topic he is preaching about for the night. Beyond all of that, Eric is an incredible man of God. You should consider bringing him in for an event.

I already had some history with Eric before this event, having partnered in ministry multiple times by this point. I first met Eric years prior on a beach in Florida for a video shoot that he was doing for a student event. When we were introduced, Eric adopted a big smile and gave me a bigger hug. As I think back on that moment, well over a decade later, I can still feel the joy that introduction brought me.

Having him at our event in Colorado was also a joy. Eric gave an incredible sermon to our junior high students. After the junior high message was done, as we waited for our high school service to begin, Eric and I had a ten-minute conversation. At first, we were doing some catching up after having not seen each other for a few years, but then, the conversation shifted toward trends we were seeing in student ministry. I shared how COVID had exacerbated an already present trend in our area toward mental health struggles for students. I could see his gears turning as we spoke, but I had no idea what was coming.

As the transition between the junior high ministry and high school ministry began, our conversation was cut short. Unbeknownst to me, Eric tucked away for the few minutes he had left before the high school service and began to pray and rework his message. Actually, rework doesn't do it justice. In the span of fifteen to twenty minutes, Eric completely rewrote his sermon for high school to directly address the growing mental health crisis from a biblical perspective. At the end of Eric's incredibly powerful sermon, he also gave an opportunity for students to respond, but he doubled down. He invited anyone whose life was specifically impacted by depression, anxiety, thoughts of suicide, or anything else related to mental health to not only raise their hand, but to get up and walk down to the front to receive prayer. We were unprepared for what came next.

Friends, it is not an exaggeration to say that 90–95 percent of our high school students went down to the front to receive prayer, well over 120 students. That moment was the convergence of years' worth of intentional effort to destigmatize mental health conversations and a powerful, Spirit-filled plea for students to not suffer alone in silence. I cannot begin to express my gratitude for Eric Samuel Timm and, more specifically, his attunement to the Holy Spirit and willingness to change direction mid-stream.

That moment was a turning point for our ministry. On one hand, we were so grateful for the grace of God to help us create a culture of psychological and emotional safety for our students to the point that so many were willing to end their silent suffering. On the other hand, we were looking out on a sea of broken, hurting, and lost students who were hungry for healing. I realized COVID had been the storm before the calm. We wept, but we also felt a collective sigh of relief because that's what happens when shame is brought into the light; it loses its power, and Jesus says, "Peace, be still." The Holy Spirit helped me see that everything was going to be okay, but we had a choice to make.

That night with Eric could have led us to go in one of two directions. The temptation we felt was to pat ourselves on the back and say, "We did it!" All of the effort was worth it. The investment had paid off. The hours of collective prayer had been answered. Thanks be to God; that's not the direction we went. By His grace, the Spirit helped us realize that it was time to double down rather than take our foot off the accelerator.

We did another parent workshop with our panel of faith-based mental health experts with the help of our co-laborers, the Johnsons. We spent even more energy training and equipping our small group leaders to help build confidence. We linked arms with other ministries in our area and collectively decided that the enemy was not going to get the last word on teen suicide in Colorado. We started doing more suicide interventions with students than before, but we took that as a sign of students feeling safe enough to ask for help, so we kept going. If COVID was the storm before the calm, this season was the continued calm before the next storm. Little did I know, the next storm would be my own.

THE STORM WITHIN ME

Then came the boulder. The season of trauma that we've discussed throughout this book began just a month and a half after Eric Samuel Timm spoke at our church. We won't rehash every detail of it here, but looking back, the timing almost makes sense. It's as if the enemy were saying, "If this guy is so hell-bent on eradicating death by suicide among students, perhaps I should undo all of God's work through him by getting *him* to die by suicide." It's honestly not a bad strategy.

Pastors, I have felt pressure to be vulnerable from the platform in the past. I know the weight and cognitive dissonance of feeling like we are supposed to be exceedingly vulnerable, and yet also come across as perfectly buttoned up at the same time. That's life in the fishbowl of ministry. This was not one of those moments. As I began my trauma therapy, I felt like I *wanted* to be vulnerable with our students and parents at an appropriate level. I mentioned before that there were concentric circles around me during this season—Mendy, family, friends, congregants, acquaintances, etc. The further out you travelled across those concentric circles, the less detail I shared, and yet there was a prompting and desire within me to push out more information about what I was going through to those circles.

I was prayerfully and carefully selective with my words. I knew there was no putting the genie back in the bottle, but on some level, I wanted and needed the genie to get out. The truth is, I am not like Lady Gaga; I have zero poker face, so people knew *something* was going on. And it felt harder not to let them know a carefully curated version of what that was. Not curated because I was trying to be dishonest, but curated because I was trying to be honoring—to myself and others who could be triggered by hearing my story. It's not easy to hear that someone you care about is struggling so much.

I first brought my church leadership into what I was going through regarding my unearthed childhood trauma. I then started trauma therapy with Brooke and, eventually, worked up to telling her all of the details of that trauma. I carefully selected friends and family to bring into the fold along the way. There were missteps. Some people weren't as safe as I thought or ready to hear what I was sharing, but overall, it felt like the more safe people I had in my corner, the safer I felt. Then, a couple of months into my trauma therapy, I shared with our students from the platform a very high-level version of what I was going through. Talk about not being able to put the genie back in the bottle . . .

My decision to share was made prayerfully and with great counsel. I processed extensively with Mendy, Brooke, and Bob across multiple weeks. The processing was fraught with anxiety, but also with glimpses of peace. I know that makes no sense, but somehow the two comingled within me to varying degrees throughout. I felt the Holy Spirit tell me, "Tomy, you have *told* students that it's safe to bring others into their struggles; this is your chance to *show* them." I am so glad I did.

Giving students a glimpse into the storm I was walking through—the storm within me—had a significant ripple effect in our ministry. I am beyond grateful for the psychological and emotional safety that was created for me by our lead team as I shared without fear of losing my job. They made me feel safe, seen, and supported in my vulnerability, and that helped me feel safe to lead from a place of vulnerability too. Leading from a place of vulnerability only multiplied the emotional and psychological safety for our students in this season. It also helped me know that I had a robust support system and an army of prayer warriors, interceding on my behalf, during my twelve-week leave of absence that summer when I was able to focus on my trauma therapy and continue seeking the healing God had in store for me. All glory to God, I came back that fall a new man. The healing was more than I could have imagined.

THE ERA OF THE SEMICOLON

The work God began in me that summer has, in many ways, continued over the subsequent years. God continues to mold me and shape me to look more like Jesus as I surrender more and more of myself to him. Formation happens over time, after all, but much of it has felt like a continuation of the trajectory God set me on during the summer of 2022. I came back that fall to some bumps in the road for our ministry as we had a couple of significant pastoral departures from our student team. But those bumps did very little to slow our momentum in our journey toward psychological safety. The Holy Spirit had the freight train rolling downhill, so we kept forging ahead.

That fall, our staff attended a faith-based suicide intervention training called Soul Shop. We gained so many new tools and ideas on how to create safety within our faith community for people to talk about their thoughts of suicide. This led me to preach a sermon to our adult congregation that directly addressed the topic of suicide. We formed even more local partnerships to provide our congregation resources, like faith-based counseling.

That was also the season we began leaning into the use of the semicolon. Remember, the semicolon represents that there is more to be written. In the written word, a semicolon tells us there is more to the story. If it were the end of the sentence, there would have been a period; God isn't done writing our stories, however, so we use a semicolon. The emergence of the semicolon visual in our ministry sought to open doors to talk to students about their mental health and, if necessary, about their season of suicidal desperation by saying as clearly as we could, "We want to help." We got every small group leader a black, hooded sweatshirt with nothing but a huge white semicolon on the front. On the back, it had our student ministry logo below a single question: "Who are your three?" This came from a concept we had learned at our Soul Shop training that encouraged us to help people identify three safe people they would reach out to if they ever had thoughts of suicide.

We encouraged students to name their three and let their three know they were listed among their safe people. The next year, the semicolon hoodies were supplemented with semicolon t-shirts as well. During those two years, students would look across a sea of people on a Sunday night at church and see it pockmarked with semicolons, inviting them to seek help if they needed it. Eventually, I would get a semicolon tattoo on my forearm as a conversation starter, and also to let others know hope is available. (Side note: If you ever see someone with a semicolon tattoo, it very likely means they have lived through a season of suicidal desperation or maybe survived instances of suicidal self-directed violence. I took a page out of my friend David's playbook, and every time I see someone with a semicolon tattoo, I say to them, "I'm glad you're here.")

The next year, I became certified as a trainer for Youth Mental Health First Aid as well as a trainer for safeTALK suicide intervention. I was also trained in ASIST, which is an even more robust tool for completing a suicide intervention and helping create a safety plan for those in places of suicidal desperation. Since then, we have taken staff members and contributors alike through those trainings to make sure they feel equipped to know how to help. We have taken some of our ushers, greeters, and prayer team members through the safeTALK training, so they can recognize the signs of someone in a place of suicidal desperation and directly ask them if they are thinking about killing themselves. We even have volunteers who have placed stickers on their lanyard name tags that say, "You can talk to me about suicide." Talk about creating psychological safety for our congregants who are experiencing suicidal ideation. I have one of those stickers on my laptop, as well, and have had several people in our community inquire.

Friends, all of these things have made such a huge difference and impact in our community. It seems daunting at first, and yet it is so very doable. It just takes time and consistency. I have now done more suicide interventions than I would care to count, and that speaks nothing of the interventions done by other staff members and volunteers. If even a percentage of those suicide interventions had not taken place, we would have likely been regularly mourning student and adult deaths by suicide over the past few years in our community. Praise God for his grace.

A FEW CAVEATS

I feel like we should pause for a moment and clarify a few things, and offer a couple of caveats. First off, if you are feeling overwhelmed at all by the effort it took to get to where our ministry is today, it's okay. Remember, you are looking at six years spread across a few pages. May looking down the road inspire you with possibilities without becoming overwhelmed. Prayerfully ask yourself and the Holy Spirit this question, "What is the next right step for our ministry in our context?" Take one step at a time through the power and guidance of the Good Shepherd, and keep in mind the heartbeat of wanting to shepherd your flock well. Pray for God to reveal who would be the right champion for this in your own ministry. You will have to stack hands as a team as you walk the path, but it will help to have someone championing this regularly—someone who already has a passion in this area who would be willing to invest some time and energy toward keeping the ball rolling.

I also want to make it abundantly clear that none of this would have been possible apart from God. I honestly wish we had been *more* intentional about bathing this whole process in prayer. About interceding on behalf of the lost, broken, and hurting. Praise God, it's never too late to raise the spiritual temperature of our ministries. Upping our prayer game is what we are actively focused on as of the writing of this book. Be sure to lean into God every step of the way. Remind yourself often that it's his power, not yours, that will make the difference.

If at any point over the past few pages it felt like we at theCREEK Student Ministry (sic) stopped preaching the gospel of Jesus in favor of preaching a gospel of mental health, then I have done a poor job of communicating our journey. Talking about mental health from the platform, far more often than not, was done in a one or two-sentence statement during a sermon about a completely different topic. It was a steady drip far more often than a heavy flow. It's the consistency that will change a culture. Remember, the Holy Spirit is our superpower, not a footnote in the story. Apart from him, we can do nothing.

I fully recognize, too, that different readers will be coming from vastly different contexts. If it sounded like the stigma was starting high for us in Colorado, I know it pales in comparison to other contexts. I've had multiple conversations with friends in Texas and Oklahoma, for instance, as they expressed their frustration and disillusionment at how much higher the stigma is in their congregations than what we were facing. I forget at times how uncomfortable conversations around mental health and suicide are for friends and family members in other parts of the country until I start talking about those topics and see them glaze over or squirm in their seats. I had grown so accustomed to sharing my story surrounding my trauma journey and having it be well-received that I was almost taken aback when I saw their discomfort manifest.

The truth is, you can only shepherd your people from wherever they currently are. Too often, the posture of the culture around us is to cancel people who don't believe or think as we do. Maybe it's a good time to remind ourselves that Jesus' harshest words were reserved for those who were self-righteous. There might need to be moments of shaking the ground and bringing challenge to those who are actively setting themselves up against our work as shepherds in this space. Far more often than not, I believe people are not being obstinate; they are merely lacking vision.

> Where there is no vision, the people perish.
> PROVERBS 29:18, KJV

In many instances, our people have been led to believe that seeing a therapist is somehow taking our eyes off of Jesus or turning to a secular source for healing rather than trusting in God. Their true desire is to keep the main thing the main thing. Honestly, that should be praised. If we can cast vision for Christian counseling and other resources as spiritual shepherding, perhaps they would make room for such options in their thinking. Perhaps they lack vision for the importance of working to keep our congregants safe, seen, and soothed.

Speaking of Christian counselors, it should be noted that not all counselors and therapists are created equal— not even all Christian counselors and therapists. It is necessary for people to do their due diligence in selecting a therapist. I reached out to several other trauma therapists before I found Brooke and felt like the Holy Spirit confirmed in my spirit that she was to be my guide. I've also worked with other therapists prior to my trauma journey, with whom I could immediately sense that they would never be my person; there was a discontent in my spirit that told me something was off. We have to learn to trust the discernment the Spirit gives us, because finding the right therapist is ultimately about trust.

We can help our sheep by doing some of the due diligence for them. I found Brooke thanks to a list of preapproved counselors and therapists on the website for Red Rocks Church in Denver. I'm incredibly grateful that they made it easy for me to find her. At Plum Creek, we now have a robust list of preapproved counselors and therapists because we've taken the time to vet them. Our goal is to make it easy by reducing friction for people to get help. For some, going to see a therapist is such a bold step of faith that it would be a shame if they started to form a relationship with a therapist only to later find out that they were getting unbiblical advice. We can help create a higher likelihood for a positive outcome by pointing them in the right direction to begin with.

Also, cast a vision for your hurting sheep that finding the right therapist or counselor can feel like dating. Some people find the right mate on their first try. Many more of us married people had to keep putting ourselves out there multiple times before we found our spouse. Let them know it's okay if the therapist doesn't feel like the right fit immediately. They can try someone else from our list. Now, at a certain point, if they have tried ten or more new options and *still* haven't found the right match, that might be communicating something else entirely. Sometimes, we are so afraid of failure or vulnerability that we self-sabotage. Sometimes, we might need to gently ask a tough question to help our hurting sheep trip over the truth that they are making excuses to not do the work that is theirs to own.

Keep encouraging people to do the work. Healing is possible. Hope is abundant. The Good Shepherd is with them, and he is with you. I know at times we can be tempted to break the legs of our sheep, so they have to stay close to us and stop falling into the same pits over and over again. But in all my research, it is clear that the idea of shepherds breaking the legs of their sheep to keep them close is not biblical; it is a myth. I get the temptation, though. I understand Moses striking the rock in the desert in a moment of frustration. The number of times I have wanted to weaponize Hebrews 5:11 against my students is staggering—look it up; I'm sure you'll understand. But God is patient with me just as he's patient with them, which reminds me that I, too, should be patient with my flock. The more I have learned to lean into the Holy Spirit, the less those feelings have come up because the fruits of patience, kindness, and gentleness are growing in me more and more.

> So let's not get tired of doing what is good. At just the right time we will reap a harvest of blessing if we don't give up.
> GALATIANS 6:9, NLT

THE CROWN OF GLORY

Friends, thank you for the work you do. Truly. The weight that comes with the mantle of leadership can be staggering. For me, when it feels too heavy, it's just a reminder that I'm trying to carry too much of the weight myself. Lean into God's Spirit. Let yourself be shepherded by the Good Shepherd. Surrender to the idea that, sometimes, we will have to work on submitting to the care and shepherding of other earthly shepherds as they speak on God's behalf. Care for yourselves well. Ask for help. You're not alone. The things of this earth—the pain, trauma, comparison, brokenness, weariness, strife, turmoil, wickedness, and sinfulness—will fade away. But the work you do for God's kingdom will last into eternity. So, shepherd well, and the crown of glory will be waiting for you.

> Be shepherds of God's flock that is under your care, watching over them . . . And when the Chief Shepherd appears, you will receive the crown of glory that will never fade away.
> 1 PETER 5:2,4

SELF-CARE AND REFLECTION

Today, I will care for myself and stay connected to God by:

Space for Reflection:

NINE

SIMPLE SELF-CARE FOR SHEPHERDS

Come away with me. Let us go alone to a quiet place and rest for a while.
MARK 6:31, WE

A PLETHORA OF 2S

I have a plethora of 2s in my life. Enneagram 2s are affectionately known as the "helpers." Helpers are the ones most likely to give you the shirt off their back and put your smallest needs above the biggest of their own. You might remember that I was raised by an Enneagram 2 mom, but there are lots of other type 2s in my life. It's hard to imagine getting better care from anyone other than a type 2. They are generous, giving, attentive, and loving. The challenge with 2s is their tendency to give and give and give until there's nothing left. It's admirable how they leave nothing in the tank, but it can lead to some long-term issues like burnout, bitterness, and compassion fatigue.

While 2s might be *most* prone to neglecting healthy practices of self-care, none of us is immune to the danger. In fact, I would argue that the number of people who are naturally good at self-care would be staggeringly low. We've said several times throughout this book that you can't pour out what isn't being poured in, and you can't take people where you haven't been yourself. This means, if we want to be in the shepherding business for the long haul, we must prioritize self-care.

Now, let me pause for just a moment to clarify what I mean by self-care. To many in the wider culture, self-care boils down to pampering, indulgence, and, at its worst, an excuse to be selfish. Scripturally, the practices we will categorize as self-care are defined as prioritizing personal health and time with the Father, so we may continue ministering to others out of his abundance. Many of the examples we see in scripture are examples of what we should *not* do, but we also have primary examples from the Good Shepherd himself on what *to* do.

The truth is, stepping into the darkness with others will sometimes bring out the darkness in us. What do we do when we ourselves are feeling overwhelmed, anxious, or empty? Shepherds need shepherding also, but *how* do we take time and energy to make sure we are marathoning and not sprinting in a way that will lead to burnout? How do we make sure we can continue to show up well for those we are shepherding? How do we take Peter's words to heart?

> Care for the flock that God has entrusted to you. Watch over it willingly, not grudgingly—not for what you will get out of it, but because you are eager to serve God.
> 1 PETER 5:2, NLT

I think it's safe to assume that none of us wants to show up for others grudgingly out of obligation. We have a desire to *want* to show up because we are eager to serve God and help others. Well, if we desire to care for the flock that God has entrusted to us, we have to learn to prioritize self-care in the same way Jesus did.

COMPASSION FATIGUE

Ask any professional caregiver, and they will tell you *compassion fatigue* is real. Compassion fatigue is simply a weariness that comes from constantly caring for others. It is a form of emotional and physical exhaustion that results from prolonged seasons of empathizing with people who are suffering or hurting to the point that we become numb. Our bodies simply were not meant to carry that kind of weight all the time. Compassion fatigue makes it difficult, if not altogether impossible, to continue to show up well for others.

Have you ever felt emotionally drained to the point of numbness? At its worst, maybe it felt hard to feel anything at all. That's your body's attempt to protect itself because there is a physical toll associated with carrying the burdens of others with them. It is your body's way of saying, "Your adrenals are shot, and we can't keep living in this heightened state forever," so it starts to shut down. The problem is that you can't stop yourself from feeling one emotion without eventually being unable to feel *any* emotion.

If you are starting to feel emotionally numb, pay attention because you are in the early stages of compassion fatigue. You will start to experience apathy toward the pain of others in ways that don't make sense *if* you notice it at all. Left unchecked, you will start to become irritable where you used to be kind and patient. You might start feeling overly cynical, asking, "What's the point? Can anyone really make a difference anyway?" Eventually, it will lead to a place of spiritual dryness. The things that used to help you feel closer to God simply won't work anymore.

An inability to feel might lead to increased isolation because you just can't deal with people anymore, because everything feels like a burden. For many, all of this will lead to escapism and engaging in numbing behaviors like doom-scrolling on social media, constantly binge-watching TV in moments of free time to drown out the silence, or maybe alcohol abuse and other risky behaviors.

If any of this sounds familiar, consider these flashing lights, warning you of the danger up ahead. It would seem Elijah didn't recognize these signs until it was too late. In 1 Kings 19, Elijah found himself in a place of suicidal desperation, or at the very least, asking God to let him die, after running to the point of exhaustion, self-isolating from his support system, and falling into the trap of comparing himself to others. At first, like Elijah, we might not recognize what we are doing to ourselves by ignoring a need for self-care and failing to turn to God early and often. Eventually, we can learn to recognize our self-destructive habits for what they are: early warning signs that we might be headed to the same place as Elijah. And once we learn to recognize them for what they are, we can follow the model Jesus gave us in Gethsemane for how to deal with overwhelm.

FOLLOW THE GOOD SHEPHERD'S EXAMPLE

Jesus was the master of self-care, which makes sense since he is the master of *everything*. Over and over again in scripture, we are told that Jesus went to a solitary place to pray. Jesus so clearly prioritized time with the Father because his humanity necessitated it. If Jesus, also fully God, prioritized time with the Father, how much more important is it for us?

What are your regular rhythms of time at the feet of Jesus? We've talked about what it might look like to prioritize time with Jesus in other chapters, but have you begun to recognize it as nonnegotiable? If you want to be the best shepherd you can be—as well as the best spouse, parent, friend, coworker, etc.—you have to make sure time with God gets prioritized in the same way Jesus did. It's not selfish, it's necessary. In fact, it's *kind* to those you care about to prioritize your own spiritual health. Take a minute to prayerfully consider how you can reclaim time in your days and weeks to spend more time at the feet of the Father. What will you give up? Screentime? TV? Podcasts? The new Taylor Swift album? Whatever it is, it will be worth it. It is time with Jesus that shapes us, refills and refuels us, sustains us, and ensures we have more to give.

As I said before, there are so many examples of Jesus prioritizing time with the Father throughout his public ministry as a means of filling up first. There is one example that stands out above the rest because there is arguably only one example in scripture of Jesus being overwhelmed and anxious. Jesus was deeply troubled and in such agony on the night of his betrayal to the point that Luke said, "His sweat became like great drops of blood falling to the ground."[1] I've been very anxious, but never sweating-drops-of-blood anxious. C.S. Lewis even pointed to Jesus' anxiety in Gethsemane as a reason for each of us to *expect* moments of feeling overwhelmed and anxious in this life.[2] The question is less about whether we feel overwhelmed and anxious and more about, "What should we do *when* we feel over-whelmed and anxious?" The answer, as is usually the case, is that we should follow the Good Shepherd's example by making space for our emotions, labeling our emotions, and turning to the Father with our emotions.

Make Space for Our Emotions

> Then Jesus went with them [his disciples] to the olive grove called Gethsemane, and he said, "Sit here while I go over there to pray." He took Peter and Zebedee's two sons, James and John, and he became anguished and distressed.
> MATTHEW 26:36-37, NLT

Jesus makes space for his emotions. It's hard to permit ourselves to deeply feel our strongest emotions in front of an audience. So, Jesus took his closest friends away from the others and let out the fullness of what he was feeling. There is something powerful about creating space to feel our feelings while inviting safe people in to see our strongest emotions. Allowing our overwhelm and anxiety to be viewed by others can be incredibly validating and healing as we are reminded that we aren't alone. Who are the safe people you could invite to carry your burdens with you? As shepherds, it's not just about carrying the burdens of others, but also about allowing other shepherds to carry ours with us as well.

Sometimes, good self-care begins with healthy boundaries. The truth is, not everyone should be invited to carry our burdens with us. We definitely need *some* people to carry our burdens with us, but not everyone. Take a moment to identify who those safe people are for you. Maybe send them a text of gratitude. If you're not sure who those people are, start by thinking about who you would *want* those safe people to be. We don't always get to choose how others prioritize us, but we can do our best to prioritize time with them and pray for God to show us the right moment to open up in some small way and gauge their response to our vulnerability. You'll probably know quickly whether or not they will be one of your safe people.

Whatever it looks like and with whomever it might happen, we have to learn to make space for our emotions, or they will come back to haunt us at some point. A quote often attributed to Sigmund Freud, the father of modern psychoanalysis, says, "Unexpressed emotions will never die. They are buried alive and will come forth later in uglier ways." You've probably experienced this. Have you ever seen someone's response to a situation be much bigger than what the situation called for? That is likely some pent-up and unexpressed emotions. Author Lysa TerKeurst popularized the phrase, "Feelings are indicators, not dictators." [3] The idea is that feelings ought to operate like a warning light on the dashboard of a car—an indicator that something under the hood needs our attention. If we let them become dictators, they move from being a warning signal to driving the car themselves, and feelings make terrible drivers. If we want our feelings to be indicators, not dictators, we have to learn, like Jesus, to make space for our emotions. After making space for his emotions and inviting his safe circle of friends to witness them, Jesus clearly labeled his emotions.

Label Our Emotions

> He told them, "My soul is crushed with grief to the point of death. Stay here and keep watch with me."
> MATTHEW 26:38, NLT

Jesus, in no uncertain terms, labeled what he was going through in that moment with very significant language. People who have been in places of suicidal desperation will understand the sentiment. It is important not only to make space for our emotions but also to clearly label our emotions. Clearly labeling our emotions gives context for understanding exactly what we are feeling and, therefore, how to proceed in processing those emotions. That can be easier said than done, though.

Emotions are complicated. Thanks to our capacity for great ambivalence—the ability to feel multiple emotions simultaneously—parsing out exactly what we are feeling will take work and maybe even professional help. There is a reason why all therapists have their own therapists. Even as professionals, we all need a guide—dare I say, a shepherd—to assist us on the journey. We all need someone to help us as we help others. Not to mention, having our own therapists can normalize and destigmatize therapy for those we are shepherding.

I know that in many Christian circles, having a therapist is seen as somehow lacking trust or faith in God as our Great Physician. Turning to a therapist in no way suggests we don't *also* turn to God. In my experience, the best therapists are those who also share our Christian worldview because they coach, counsel, and shepherd us *toward* God. I remember multiple times during my intensive, Kelley pausing to pray or taking her shoes off because it felt like we were entering holy ground. My therapists have helped *strengthen* my dependence on Jesus, not replace my dependence on him. Brooke, Kelley, and Dr. Jess (my neuropsychologist who has helped me with continued healing from my traumatic brain injury) have all reinforced Jesus as my true source of healing. Maybe it's time to find your own professional

Christian shepherd, so they can help you label your emotions and sort out the complicated web of feelings you carry.

Apart from a good Christian counselor, one of my favorite resources in this space is Brené Brown's book *Atlas of the Heart*, which defines eighty-seven unique emotions! As the term *atlas* suggests, it operates like a roadmap, helping you find the right label for the right emotion that you might be feeling. For me, it has been wildly helpful to have so much language to help label my emotions, because it helps me understand exactly what I am going through and how to sit with that specific emotion. Whatever tool you use—therapist, book, feelings wheel, etc.—following the example of the Good Shepherd means learning to label your emotions and asking safe people to sit with you in those emotions. Finally, after making space for his emotions and labeling his emotions, Jesus turned to God the Father.

Run to The Father

He went on a little farther and bowed with his face to the ground, praying, "My Father! If it is possible, let this cup of suffering be taken away from me. Yet I want your will to be done, not mine."
Matthew 26:39, NLT

Jesus showed us the importance of turning to the Father in moments of overwhelm and anxiousness. He went straight to his own source of life, strength, and peace in a moment when all of them were on shaky ground, to say the least. Not only did he turn to the Father, but he made a clear ask: if possible, take it away! Notice that he wasn't asking God to take away his *anxiousness*, but to take away the impending agonizing *pain* of crucifixion, the unbearable *weight* of the world, and the unfathomable *separation* that would happen for the first time between Jesus and God the Father as he would take on the sins of the world. Essentially, this was Jesus asking, "Are we sure this has to be the path toward reconciliation and redemption for all humanity?"

None of us will ever know the weight Jesus was about to carry, and yet as shepherds, we all know—or at least one day *will* know—the weight of carrying the burdens of others with them. Left to our own strength, the weight is crushing. But be reminded, when we cry out to Jesus on their behalf and ours as well, we are asking Jesus to carry the weight with and for us. Unless we run to the Father regularly with the weights we carry, they will consume us. But when we rely on the strength of the Holy Spirit rather than our own—as well as the collective strength of our support systems—the weights become manageable. Psalm 91 says it this way:

> Those who live in the shelter of the Most High will find rest in the shadow of the Almighty. This I declare about the LORD: He alone is my refuge, my place of safety; he is my God, and I trust him.
> PSALM 91:1-2, NLT

Friends, when we get to a place of feeling overwhelmed and anxious, may we follow the example of our Good Shepherd and create space for our emotions, label our emotions, and turn to the Father with our emotions. He alone is our source of strength. He alone can renew us and sustain us. Ignoring our emotions of overwhelm, anxiety, grief, anguish, etc., will only serve to burn us out or lead to a place of compassion fatigue. There are also practices we can learn to prevent feeling overwhelmed as often—a choose your own adventure of sorts.

CHOOSE YOUR OWN ADVENTURE

As a kid, I loved to read Choose Your Own Adventure books. If you've never had the pleasure, let me paint a picture of how they work. For a few pages, the author sucks you into the story, and then, at random intervals, you are given options as to what you would like to see the hero of the story do next. It will say something like, "If you want our hero to go into the cave, keep reading. If you want our hero to choose the mountain path, turn to page seventeen. If you want our hero to summon a fire eagle, turn to page thirty-eight." I'm not sure these are great options, but you get the idea. Choose your own adventure novels give you the chance to participate in the story in a way that allows you to influence the outcomes.

A good self-care plan has to operate like a Choose Your Own Adventure novel, because there is no one-size-fits-all formula for spiritual formation. We are all wired in different ways, which means we all connect to God in different ways. Sure, there are some basic building blocks (think back to "The Nine" from chapter six), but how we use them will be vastly different based on a host of factors. We should all be reading our Bibles in some way, shape, or form because "The word of God is living and active, sharper than any two-edged sword."[4] I can't imagine trying to follow Jesus without knowing what Jesus said. And yet, *how* we best read in order to get the most out of time in our Bibles can vary drastically from person to person. Some love reading multiple chapters of the Bible in one sitting, while others prefer spending days at a time meditating on a single verse. Some sit with open commentaries and study various translations covering their entire table, while others find power in listening to the Bible in audio form while they move their bodies. It's about finding what works for you.

That is why the following will be a far-from-exhaustive list of self-care ideas to get your wheels turning. Try some on. See what fits. Come up with your own. Ask other shepherds you admire what they do. It will likely take time to hone in on what you need for this particular season, but don't give up, even if it feels clunky at first. Remember, it's too important *not* to do it. I have utilized every form of self-care on this list at one time or another to ensure I have the energy to continue shepherding, and I hope these ideas will help you too.

Physical

- **Practice breathing exercises.** There are many versions out there. Do a quick internet search and learn more about box breathing, pursed lips breathing, belly breathing, etc.
- **Move your body.** This might be exercise, going outside, touching grass, or stretching. Anything to get your blood flowing, and a change of scenery almost always helps reset the brain. The best version is coupling that movement with prayer in some way.
- **Choose healthy diet options.** The sugar and unhealthy fats in junk food might provide an immediate spike, but almost always leave us feeling worse once the effects wear off.
- **Rest without guilt.** Sleep, recreation, and margin are spiritual disciplines. We were never meant to maximize and fill every single moment of every single day. You never once see Jesus in a hurry. Maybe we should take our cues from him.

Spiritual

- **Retreat regularly**. Find daily, weekly, monthly, and yearly moments of sabbath. Build a regular rhythm of sacred pauses into your life, and you'll be surprised how much more you hear from God. Go on a retreat, take a walk, touch grass, or spend unhurried time with family.
- **Pray.** Try new types of prayer like praying the psalms, breath prayers, centering prayers, etc.
- **Listen to worship music.** Few things recenter me as much as choosing to worship in song during a low moment.
- **Memorize scripture**. I was never very intentional about this until recently, and it has been a game-changer. In fact, as of the writing of this book, I have memorized about 180 verses in a little over a year. Want to know how? I replaced

doom scrolling with scripture memorization during my time on the toilet. Turns out I have a lot more extra time on my hands than I thought. If you need more time, eat more fiber.

- **Read *Sacred Pathways*.** Seriously, do it. Gary Thomas' book will open your eyes to new ways of connecting with God that you've probably never thought about.

Mental

- **Practice mindfulness.** Practice becoming aware of your surroundings. What do you smell? What do you see? What do you hear? Thanks to DiFab (see chapter three), I recently got into birdwatching as a way to slow down and become more present when I'm outside. It has made a big difference.
- **Capture thoughts.** Learn to become aware of your internal dialogue and control where it goes rather than letting your thoughts run wild. The best thing we can do is turn to relevant truth in God's Word when our thoughts are wreaking havoc.
- **Practice Meditation.** In his book *Celebration of Discipline*, Richard Foster points out that Christian meditation and Eastern meditation are not the same thing. Eastern meditation is about emptying our minds, whereas Christian meditation is about filling our minds with God.
- **Find a Christian therapist.** There's no shame in shepherds finding a shepherd.

Emotional

- **Reflect Honestly.** I've never consistently journaled, but I have friends and family members who swear by it. For me, it looks less like writing it down and more like taking time to silently reflect on my days and weeks in prayer.

- **Do a feelings check.** Set an alarm throughout your day, and when it goes off, take time to label your emotions. Bonus points for pausing long enough to trace those feelings back to their source.

Intellectual

- **Read a book.** Reduce your screen time by an hour each week and replace it with reading.
- **Do a puzzle.** For real, puzzles are the best. They slow you down and challenge you mentally while also creating space to think and process, or else have a great conversation with whoever is doing the puzzle with you.
- **Try a new hobby.** Learning something new fires up the old neurons in your brain in ways that can be life-giving and refreshing.

Social

- **Prioritize time for life-giving relationships.** Call or text a friend you haven't seen in a while. Go for coffee with your favorite encourager. Write a note of appreciation to your support system. Play disc golf with Taylor—ok, maybe that one was more for me than you.
- **Receive from others.** It's okay to let others shepherd you. In fact, you need it. Isolation isn't holiness; it's hazardous. Find spaces where you can show up without an expectation to lead.
- **Learn to say no.** Take time to read Lysa TerKeurst's book *Your Best Yes*. It will give you a framework for why you should say *no* to some things, so you can say your best *yes* to the most important things.

Again, be reminded that these are just a few options out of a virtually limitless sea of self-care practices. Identify a few, schedule them, practice them, and see what happens. Maybe they will help increase your emotional capacity as you prioritize time with God and practices that fill your cup; they certainly filled my cup when I started practicing self-care regularly. Whatever it looks like, find ways to replenish yourself, so you can effectively shepherd others. It's not selfish, it's necessary.

MORE IS CAUGHT THAN TAUGHT

In our student ministry world, we often say more is caught than taught. In fact, that's the title of the podcast we make for the parents of our students: "More is Caught Than Taught." It's a reminder that the very thing that will help others live out of truth more than anything else is seeing us as their shepherds, living out of truth. Go ahead and say it with me: "We can't take people further than we've been ourselves." So, we have to make sure we are doing our own work to live no lies and stay close to Jesus.

The best form of witness is a life bathed in grace, close to Jesus, and in tune with the Spirit. As shepherds, this is the kind of life we are inviting sheep to join us in living, which means it *has* to be the kind of life we are wholeheartedly pursuing for ourselves. Pastor and author Brennan Manning famously said, "The greatest single cause of atheism in the world today is Christians who acknowledge Jesus with their lips, then walk out the door and deny him by their lifestyle. That is what an unbelieving world simply finds unbelievable."[5] Inviting the hurting into a life that we ourselves are not living will create cognitive dissonance. This doesn't mean we have to be perfect before we can shepherd others, but it *does* mean we will have very little credibility if they see vast inconsistencies in our words and actions.

If we ourselves are prioritizing time with Jesus that we may become more like him and do as he did, shepherding becomes much simpler. All that is required of us is presence. As we've said consistently throughout this book, we are hope incarnate because we carry with us the very presence of the Holy Spirit wherever we go. Spending time with the hurting will expose them to the Jesus reflected by our lives, that *they* may become more like him and do as he did.

> Let your light shine before others, that they may see your good deeds and glorify your Father in heaven.
> MATTHEW 5:16

If it is true that more is caught than taught, and I firmly believe it is, perhaps the best thing you can do for those who are hurting is be with them in authenticity and vulnerability. Prioritize time with Jesus, and you will always have something to give away. Lean into the Holy Spirit, and you will always carry the healing presence with you. Submit to the Father, and you will find that your worth is not in your work, but in his unwavering delight in you. Let him fill what emptiness remains, still your hurried heart, and remind you that the Shepherd who called you to this work is the same one who carries you when you're weary. Rest in his care, so your care for others flows from overflow, not exhaustion. Remember, self-care for a shepherd isn't selfish; it's stewardship. The more you let yourself be tended by the Good Shepherd, the more faithfully you can tend to those entrusted to your care.

SELF-CARE AND REFLECTION

Today, I will care for myself and stay connected to God by:

Space for Reflection:

EPILOGUE

THE GREAT COMMISSION

I f you are a follower of Jesus, you are a shepherd. We established as much all the way back in the Introduction. Jesus already commissioned you to make disciples. For many people, part of that discipleship journey is walking through significant seasons of pain. Lamenting the loss of loved ones. Walking through mental health struggles. Learning to root their identities in Christ by unraveling the lies of the enemy. We all need a shepherd, and the good news is that we all *have* a Shepherd. As the Good Shepherd cares for you, he has also commissioned you to turn around and shepherd others.

And so, as we near the end of our time together through this book, I want to offer you a reminder of that commissioning in the form of a blessing. Blessings in the Bible were powerful and strategically chosen words that cast a vision of a preferred future of complete surrender to God the Father. They were uniquely tailored to speak truth, love, and hope into and over the lives of those receiving the blessing. The job of the hearer is to receive the blessing. To let it take root in their hearts and minds in a way that would shape their way forward.

If possible, I would encourage you to place your hands palms up in front of you in a posture of receiving as you prop open the book and read it. If that's not possible, perhaps you could invite someone close to you to read it over you, or else you can go to the resources page at www.shepherdsofthemind.com, and it will be my honor to read it over you from your device. Take a deep breath, invite the Holy Spirit to open your heart, and receive. And so, dear shepherds, a blessing:

Shepherds,

May you walk closely with the One who knows his sheep by name.

May you make yourself available as he uses you to call his other sheep by name into a life of healing and wholeness.

May you be deeply aware of the presence of the Holy Spirit that you carry with you into sacred spaces of pain.

May you be wildly attuned to the promptings of the Spirit as you go about your days.

May you be abundantly obedient when the Spirit moves you.

May your hands be gentle, not because you are weak, but because you know the strength of mercy.

May your voice echo the tone of the Shepherd-King—never hurried, never harsh, always gentle with the hurting.

May you remember that it is not your job to save, but to show up. Not to fix, but to follow. Not to carry the weight of outcomes, but to bear the weight of obedience.

May you be the kind of presence that helps the hurting feel safe again.

May you be quick to listen, slow to speak, and always ready to stay through the silence.

May you abide in the Shepherd even as you tend to his sheep.

And may his Spirit renew your strength when you grow tired, restore your soul when it grows thin, and remind you again and again that you are being shepherded too.

Go now, not as the hero of anyone's story, but as the hands and feet of the One who laid down his life for the sheep.

He is the Good Shepherd. And he is very, very good.

Amen.

FINAL REFLECTION

Shepherds, I encourage you to take some time to look back on all of your reflections throughout this book. Prayerfully consider the following prompts:

- What themes have emerged during your times of reflection?
- What do you believe God is calling you to do in this next season as you seek to shepherd others on their mental health journeys?
- What rhythms and practices do you need to adopt to ensure that you are ready to shepherd others for the long haul?
- What next steps will you take to further educate yourself so you feel prepared and confident in your ability to shepherd others through the power of the Holy Spirit?

APPENDIX A

DISCLAIMER

While this book offers tools, stories, and spiritual guidance, it cannot replace the wisdom, care, and support of trained mental health professionals. The practices in these pages are meant to help you show up with compassion, not to diagnose, treat, or assume the role of a clinician.

Your role is to care like Christ, offer presence, and help connect others to the appropriate professionals who are equipped to provide medical and therapeutic support.

If you are struggling, please seek a licensed therapist, counselor, psychiatrist, or medical provider. Your life is worth protecting. Your pain is not the end of your story. Hope and help are available today.

IF YOU ARE IN CRISIS

If you are thinking about harming yourself, or if you feel unsafe in any way, please seek help immediately. You do not need to walk through this moment alone.

If you are in immediate danger

- Call 911
- Or go to the nearest emergency room

If you are having thoughts of suicide or self-harm

- Call or text 988 (the Suicide & Crisis Lifeline)
- If you're outside of the United States, please contact your local emergency number or crisis hotline.

If you are not in immediate danger but need support

- Reach out to a trusted friend, family member, pastor, or counselor right away.
- Tell someone what you're feeling. You don't have to explain it perfectly. Simply saying, "I'm not okay," is enough to start getting help.
- You may feel overwhelmed, afraid, or ashamed, but those feelings do not define you. Reaching out for help is a courageous step toward healing. The Good Shepherd draws near to the brokenhearted, and there are people ready to walk with you right now.

DISCERNING MANIPULATION

Sadly, there are instances where some will use threats of suicide as a manipulation tactic. I have firsthand experience of situations where expressions of suicidal intent became intertwined with relational pressure, leaving caregivers unsure about how to respond without feeling emotionally cornered. These moments require both compassion and clarity because, while the pain may be real, responding without boundaries can ultimately do more harm than good. Naming this reality is not meant to minimize the seriousness of suicidal language—every mention of suicide should always be taken seriously

—but it is meant to help us respond wisely rather than reactively. When suicide is used as leverage, the goal is often control or avoidance rather than a genuine intent to die. Even so, the response should remain the same: take the words seriously, refuse to negotiate under threat, and involve appropriate support.

Do not argue about whether they *really mean it*. Do not promise secrecy. Do not allow yourself to be isolated as the sole source of care. Instead, calmly say something like, "I care about you too much to handle this alone. Because you're talking about suicide, we need to bring in more support to help keep you safe." Then, follow through—loop in trusted family members, church leadership, or mental health professionals as appropriate. Healthy care draws boundaries around manipulation without withdrawing compassion. You can be kind without being controlled. You can be present without being trapped. And you can love someone well while still recognizing when the situation requires help beyond what you can offer on your own.

APPENDIX B

A QUICK REFERENCE GUIDE TO SEEK

<u>S</u> – *Spot the Signs*
Look for clues in what they say, how they act, or what they're facing.

- Statements of wanting to disappear or feeling hopeless
- Withdrawal from people or activities
- Giving away prized possessions
- Making arrangements for pets or loved ones
- Major life stressors, losses, or shame

If the signs are present, don't ignore them.

<u>E</u> – *Evaluate the Risk*
Ask the direct question, "Are you thinking about killing yourself?" If
they say yes, ask gentle clarifying questions to discern if they have a
plan, if they have gathered means, and if they have decided when. This
will help you understand urgency.

E – Engage with Empathy

Your presence matters more than perfect words. Give them a chance to share their story if they want to, and say things like:

"I'm so sorry for the pain you're carrying."
"Thank you for trusting me."
"You are not alone."

Avoid minimizing or trying to fix. Listen, stay present, and create safety.

K – Keep Them Safe

- Stay with them—don't leave them alone.
- Remove access to lethal means if safe to do so.
- Call or text 988 together, or call 911 if the risk is immediate.
- Help them connect with trained professionals.

If necessary, offer to take them to the hospital. Keeping someone alive in the moment is the most important step.

APPENDIX C
KEY TERMS

Mental Health & Emotional Well-Being

Mental Health
A person's overall emotional, psychological, and social well-being—how they think, feel, and act, and how they handle stress, relate to others, and make decisions. Mental health exists on a spectrum and can fluctuate over time.

Mental Health Crisis
A moment or season in which a person's thoughts, feelings, or behaviors put them at risk of harming themselves or others, or when the intensity of distress makes normal functioning difficult. Crises require presence, support, and often, immediate intervention.

Trauma
An emotional or psychological wound, caused when an experience overwhelms a person's ability to cope. Trauma may be:

- Acute (single event)

- Chronic (repeated or ongoing)
- Complex (relational or developmental harm over time)

Trauma is not just what happened *to* a person but what happened *inside* them in the aftermath.

Post-Traumatic Stress / PTSD
Stress reactions following trauma that may include flashbacks, intrusive memories, nightmares, emotional numbness, or hypervigilance. When these symptoms persist and impair life for over a month, PTSD may be diagnosed.

Thoughts, Feelings & Internal Experiences

Anxiety
Persistent worry, fear, or tension that becomes difficult to control and interferes with daily functioning. Often accompanied by physical symptoms like restlessness, rapid heartbeat, or difficulty sleeping.

Depression
A prolonged state of sadness, emptiness, or loss of interest. Depression affects thinking, energy, sleep, appetite, and hope. It is not simply "feeling down."

Panic Attack
A sudden surge of intense fear or discomfort that peaks within minutes, often accompanied by symptoms such as rapid, shallow breathing, chest pain, trembling, dizziness, or a sense of losing control.

Intrusive Thoughts
Unwanted, involuntary thoughts, images, or impulses that may feel disturbing or out of character. Intrusive thoughts do not indicate a person wants to act on them; they reflect distress, not desire.

Dissociation
A sense of disconnection from one's thoughts, body, or surroundings
—often a protective response to overwhelming stress or trauma.

Shame
A painful belief that one is unworthy, unlovable, or fundamentally
flawed. Guilt says, "I did something wrong." Shame says, "I am something wrong."

Self-Harm & Suicide-Related Terms

Self-Harm / Non-Suicidal Self-Injury
Intentional self-inflicted harm (such as cutting or burning) used to
cope with overwhelming emotional pain. While not always a suicide
attempt, it is always a sign of deep distress.

Suicidal Ideation
Thoughts about death or suicide.

- **Passive:** "I wish I wouldn't wake up."
- **Active:** "I'm thinking about ending my life."

Both are serious and require care and connection.

Suicide Attempt / Suicidal Self-Directed Violence
An act of self-directed violence with the intent to die. Surviving an
attempt is a pivotal moment that requires compassionate support and
follow-up care.

Protective Factors
Characteristics or resources that reduce the likelihood of suicide or
crisis: faith, healthy relationships, belonging, professional support,
hope, purpose, and connection.

Risk Factors
Circumstances or conditions that increase suicide vulnerability: past attempts, trauma history, isolation, substance use, chronic pain, access to lethal means, and intense feelings of worthlessness or hopelessness.

Relationship, Community & Shepherding Terms

Presence
The ministry of showing up. A calm, non-anxious, attentive companionship that communicates, "You are not alone." Presence is more healing than perfect words.

Psychological Safety
A relational environment where a person feels safe to be honest without fear of judgment, disbelief, or shame. Psychological safety is the soil where confession, lament, and healing can grow.

Safe Space
A place—physical or relational— where someone can express struggles, feelings, or questions without fear of rejection or minimizing.

Compassion Fatigue
Emotional exhaustion and reduced capacity for empathy can develop from prolonged exposure to the suffering of others. Often affects pastors, caregivers, and helpers.

Burnout
A state of emotional, physical, and mental exhaustion caused by prolonged stress or overwork. Burnout signals a need for rest, margin, and soul renewal.

Spiritual Formation & Biblical Concepts

Lament
A biblical practice of bringing grief, confusion, pain, and questions honestly before God. Lament holds sorrow and trust together and turns suffering into prayer.

Spiritual Formation
The lifelong process of being shaped into the image of Christ for the sake of others. Mental and emotional health are inseparable from this journey.

Shalom
A Hebrew word meaning peace, harmony, completeness, and flourishing. Shalom is not merely the absence of conflict, but the presence of wholeness with God, others, self, and creation.

Practical Care Concepts

Grounding Techniques
Simple exercises (breathing, sensory focus, name-five-things method) that help someone regain calm, reorient to the present, and regulate overwhelming emotions.

Deescalation
Ways of responding that help a distressed person move toward calm: soft tone, slow pace, open posture, validation, curiosity, and non-judgment.

Referral
Encouraging someone to seek professional support—counseling, therapy, or pastoral care—when needs exceed your role or expertise. Referral is not passing someone off; it's shepherding wisely.

DISCUSSION QUESTIONS
FOR GROUPS

INTRODUCTION — SHEEP WITHOUT A SHEPHERD

1. Tomy describes the enemy using shame to isolate people in their darkest seasons. Where have you seen this dynamic in yourself or others?
2. The Introduction frames "presence, not perfection" as the foundation of shepherding. What does this look like practically in your context?
3. What phrases or moments from Tomy's trauma story stood out to you the most and why?
4. Who has been a "wounded healer" in your life? What made their presence meaningful?
5. Which part of Ezekiel 34:4 feels most important in your setting right now?
6. What fears do you have about walking with someone through a mental health crisis?
7. Where do you sense God inviting you to greater availability rather than ability?

1. LEAD GENTLY

1. Tomy writes that gentleness creates emotional safety. What does emotional safety feel like to you?
2. Think of a time someone "led you gently." What did they do that made a difference?
3. Where do you tend to lean—toward *all support* (enabling) or *all challenge* (domineering)? Why?
4. How do you normally respond when someone else's pain makes you uncomfortable?
5. What practical habits help you slow down, listen deeply, and hold space?
6. Which example of Jesus' compassion resonated with you most?
7. Tomy says, "Don't forget your superpower: the Holy Spirit." What might it look like to rely on the Spirit more intentionally when caring for others?

2. SEEK THE LOST

1. How did reading about the "un-askable question" impact you emotionally?
2. What makes it difficult for many people to talk honestly about suicide?
3. Which definitions (ideation, desperation, intrusive thoughts, etc.) were clarifying or surprising?
4. How does scripture's portrayal of suicidal despair challenge common Christian misunderstandings?
5. What helps you discern when someone might be silently drowning?
6. What holds you back from asking hard, direct questions when someone is struggling?

7. How might God be calling you to seek someone who feels lost right now?

3. ROUND UP THE STRAYS

1. Why do hurting people often isolate themselves from community, even when they need it most?
2. When you think of "strays," who comes to mind—not as a project, but as a person you love?
3. What relational behaviors in yourself might unintentionally push straying people further away?
4. What is the difference between *pursuing someone* and *pressuring someone*?
5. Describe a time when you felt gently pursued but didn't know how to return.
6. What is one practice you could adopt to help someone feel seen without feeling chased?
7. How might Jesus pursue the person in your life who is currently drifting?

4. BIND UP THE INJURED

1. What kinds of "injuries" (emotional, spiritual, relational) are most difficult for you to sit with?
2. What are the signs that someone is in immediate emotional pain that requires presence, not solutions?
3. Tomy writes that people need to be *felt* before they can be helped. How have you seen that ring true?
4. What stops us from entering someone's pain without rushing to fix it?
5. What does "sitting in the suck" look like in real life?
6. Which of your relationships currently need your patient presence?

7. How does Jesus model entering pain rather than avoiding it?

5. HEAL THE SICK

1. How does misplaced identity contribute to ongoing emotional or spiritual sickness?
2. What truths about identity in Christ feel hardest for people to believe during a crisis?
3. How can you speak truth without minimizing someone's experience or emotions?
4. Which "sick" patterns (shame, fear, destructive narratives) do you see most often in your ministry or relationships?
5. What has helped you replace lies with truth?
6. How did Jesus balance honesty with tenderness in his healing interactions?
7. What identity-based truths might God be inviting you to share with someone?

6. STRENGTHEN THE WEAK

1. What does weakness look like in the context of long-term recovery or discipleship?
2. How can you help someone build resilience without placing unrealistic expectations on them?
3. Which spiritual practices bring you strength in seasons of exhaustion or discouragement?
4. What happens when you try to "strengthen" someone before you've first been present in their pain?
5. How do community rhythms (confession, encouragement, Sabbath, accountability) strengthen the vulnerable?
6. Who has strengthened you when you were weak and how?

7. Where might God be asking you to invest long-term, patient strengthening in another person?

7. YOUR GOOD SHEPHERD

1. Which aspect of Jesus as the Good Shepherd is most comforting to you?
2. Where do you struggle to trust his shepherding in your own story?
3. How does understanding Jesus' presence reshape how we show up for others?
4. What does it look like to rest rather than strive in shepherding?
5. How has God used your past pain to help shepherd someone else?
6. In what ways do you feel the Shepherd inviting you into deeper dependence today?
7. How might this chapter shift the way you view your role in discipleship?

8. A TALE OF REDEMPTION

1. What part of the redemption story shared in this chapter moved you most deeply?
2. What does this redemption story teach us about God's patience and timing?
3. Where have you witnessed God bringing beauty from ashes —either in you or someone you shepherded?
4. How does redemption reshape identity, confidence, or calling?
5. What false beliefs tend to resurface as you walk toward healing?

6. Where do you want to see redemption break forth in your life today?
7. How can your redemption become a resource for others without putting yourself at the center?

9. SIMPLE SELF-CARE FOR SHEPHERDS

1. Which self-care practices feel natural to you? Which feels like work?
2. What emotions surface when you consider caring for yourself with the same compassion you give others?
3. How do you discern the difference between rest and avoidance?
4. What warning signs signal that your emotional or spiritual reserves are running low?
5. How has helping others in crisis affected your well-being?
6. What boundaries might help you shepherd more sustainably?
7. Which self-care practice do you want to try this week?

GRATITUDE

Writing this book has been one of the most meaningful and stretching experiences of my life, and it would not exist without the people who shepherded me even as I sought to learn how to shepherd others.

To my wife Mendy: thank you for your patience, encouragement, and steady presence through every late night, every moment of self-doubt, and every heavy lift with the kiddos so I could go on writer's retreats. Thanks for asking the hard question and showing me what psychological safety truly is. Your own journey into the world of counseling has sharpened my heart and imagination for this work. You are the bravest and most compassionate person I know, and I'm endlessly grateful to walk through life with you. Skies could be blue...

To my kids, Laney Drew and Judah James: you bring joy into every corner of my world. Thank you for reminding me, simply by being yourselves, that tenderness, curiosity, and laughter are essential parts of healing. You are a bold, bright light for Jesus in this dark world and a reminder of his grace and truth at work in my life. I hope someday you'll read this book and know that you shaped it in ways you don't even realize.

To Eric Samuel Timm, thank you for lending your voice to the foreword, being a voice for encouragement through the years, and showing up in a pivotal moment of our ministry's journey. Your authenticity, courage, and commitment to sharing the gospel well have inspired me more than you know. Keep painting hope.

To my sister Cristina: thank you for being both my editor and my sounding board throughout this entire process. You helped me clarify ideas, refine language, and say things the way I *meant* to say them. Your insight, patience, and attention to detail strengthened this book in ways readers may never see, but I always will. I'm grateful beyond words for your support and for the gift you are in my life.

To my friends and mentors through the years: Travis Janzen, Blair Spindle, David Frisbie, Bob Seale, the Wolf Pack, the Weekend Leapfroggers, our home group, and others who have cheered me on. Thank you for showing me the heart of the Good Shepherd and for believing in me even in the seasons when I struggled to believe in myself.

To my friend and co-laborer in eradicating deaths by suicide in Colorado, David Galvan: your heart for the hurting is inspiring, and your friendship is invaluable. You started me on this journey of suicide intervention, and this book simply does not exist without you. Keep up the great work of equipping others to show up for the lost and hurting.

To Doug, Bob, Craig, Eric, and the board of Plum Creek Church: thank you for creating a culture where mental health is not taboo but tenderly acknowledged, prayed over, and cared for. Your care for me before, during, and after my trauma journey played a significant role in the healing the Holy Spirit brought to my family and me. Your commitment to shepherding well has given life to this book.

To Jenna and the many others who have been part of our student team at Plum Creek Church: thank you for shepherding well and helping create psychological safety for our students. Your care for others is second to none, and your care for my family and me has been a huge factor in my longevity in ministry.

To the students of Plum Creek Church: you are the reason I care so deeply about this message. You've trusted me with your questions, your fears, your pain, and your stories. You've shown me over and over that teenagers are not the future of the church; you are the vibrant, courageous heartbeat of the church right now. Keep pursuing Jesus well until it is in Castle Rock as it is in heaven.

To the mental health professionals who helped shape this work: Veronica Johnson for your partnership in ministry and for being my beta reader and offering feedback on an early draft of this book; Brooke, Kelley, and Jess who have walked with me and shepherded me toward healing in the name of the Good Shepherd, and every trainer who has led me through YMHFA, TMHFA, safeTALK, ASIST, Soul Shop, and QPRT, to all of you: thank you. Your wisdom and compassion have saved lives, including mine.

To Nancy and Chef Mr. Gene: thank you for your steady care and friendship through the years and for the generous gift of your condo during my sabbatical. It was profoundly fitting to begin writing this book at the very table where I received such meaningful care during my trauma journey. And to the Dawsons: thank you for opening your cabin to me for a writing retreat—the quiet space where the first full draft of this book finally came together on the fourth anniversary of my Stay Day. The generosity of each of you created sacred space for healing work and holy work alike, and I'm deeply grateful.

To the broader family of pastors, authors, and thinkers whose ideas echo throughout these pages: N.T. Wright, Dallas Willard, Curt Thompson, Steve Carter, Henry Cloud, John Townsend, Michael John Cusick, and so many others, thank you for helping me see the Shepherd more clearly and for giving language to what my heart was trying to say.

And finally, to the Good Shepherd, who finds me, carries me, restores me, and sends me to do the same. Every story of healing in these pages is his story, not mine. May this book serve his purposes and reflect his heart.

NOTES

Introduction

1. John Mark Comer, *Practicing the Way: Be with Jesus, Become like Him, Do as He Did* (WaterBrook, 2024).
2. See Philippians 3:20.

1. Lead Gently

1. Polaroid cameras instantly print a picture straight from the camera itself. Also, if you are reading this endnote, you were for SURE born after 2000 so you should also check out some other 1900s nostalgia like Trapper Keepers, Pogs, and the GOAT (Greatest Of All Time): Michael Jordan.
2. For more on the Enneagram, I recommend Ian Morgan Cron and Suzanne Stabile's, *The Road Back to You: An Enneagram Journey to Self-Discovery,* or Cron's "Typology" podcast.
3. Ian Morgan Cron and Suzanne Stabile, *The Road Back to You: An Enneagram Journey to Self-Discovery,* (InterVarsity Press, 2016), 15.
4. John Calvin, *Institutes of the Christian Religion,* trans. Ford Lewis Battles, ed. John T. McNeill (Westminster John Knox Press, 1960), I.i.1.
5. Mark 1:40-41, NLT.
6. See John 9.
7. See John 4:1-38.
8. See John 8:1-11.
9. See Luke 19:1-10.
10. Matthew 14:31.
11. See Luke 24:36-37.
12. John 8:11.
13. John 8:11, NLT.
14. For more on the Support-Challenge Matrix, check out *The 100X Leader,* by Jeremie Kubiceck & Steve Cockram (John Wiley & Sons, Inc., 2019).
15. 1 Corinthians 13:5.
16. These are lyrics from the song *Bright Sadness* by Sleeping at Last.
17. Celebrate Recovery is a Christ-centered, Twelve step addiction recovery program.
18. My favorite resource on apology is, *The Five Languages of Apology: How to Experience Healing in All Your Relationships* by Gary Chapman and Jennifer M. Thomas (Northfield Publishing, 2006).
19. For a dramatized retelling of this story, go to www.shepherdsofthemind.com.
20. I would HIGHLY recommend checking out *The Practice of The Presence of God and The Way of Perfection* By Brother Lawrence and Teresa of Avila (Thomas Nelson Inc, 1999).

2. Seek the Lost

1. In Acts 1:18-19, Judas' death appears to be more accidental as it describes him falling headlong and his intestines spilling out. Many scholars interpret these two accounts as different perspectives of the same event, suggesting he hanged himself and then, as the branch broke or his body decomposed, he fell and split open.

2. I am trained in the National Council for Mental Wellbeing's YMHFA (Youth Mental Health First Aid) and TMHFA (Teen Mental Health First Aid), Living-Works' safeTALK, LivingWorks Asist, Soul Shop, and QPRT Suicide Risk Detection.

3. Edwin S. Shneidman, *The Suicidal Mind* (New York: Oxford University Press, 1996).

4. You can find Kevin's story on YouTube or by watching the documentary *Suicide: The Ripple Effect.*

5. Harvard T.H. Chan School of Public Health, www. execedonline.hsph.harvard.e-du/global-public-health-leadership-program?utm_source=bing&utm_medi-um=c&utm_location=91135&utm_campaign=B-365D_US_BG_SE_HPH-GPH.SEPO_Brand&utm_content=GPH-Brand&utm_term=har-vard%20t%20h%20chan%20school%20of%20pub-lic%20health&msclkid=9a2971c915f11a7330067189bbd262986.

6. Youth Mental Health First Aid, training slide deck, National Council for Mental Wellbeing, 2025.

7. Ronald C. Kessler et al., "Prevalence, Severity, and Comorbidity of 12-Month DSM-IV Disorders in the National Comorbidity Survey Replication (NCS-R)," *Archives of General Psychiatry* 62, no. 6 (2005), 617–627.

8. Valerie J. Callanan and Mark S. Davis, "Gender Differences in Suicide Methods," *Social Psychiatry and Psychiatric Epidemiology* 47, no. 6 (2012), 857–869.

9. Nock M.K., Borges G, Bromet EJ et al. Br J. Psychiatry 2008;192:98-105.

10. ten Have M, de Graaf R., van Dorsselaer S. et al. Can J Psychiatry 2009;54:824-33.

11. It's unclear in my research where this hermeneutical connection originated. I first heard my friend, David Galvan, connect Acts 16:28 to modern day suicide intervention efforts at a Soul Shop Faith-Based Suicide Intervention workshop. It was brought to my attention as I wrote this book that author and pastor Steve Carter has made the same connection multiple times as well across multiple sermons. Regardless of where it originated, I am grateful and hope more pastors will continue to preach hope through this same hermeneutical interpretation of scripture.

12. For more information, visit www.soulshopmovement.org.

3. Round up the Strays

1. Charles H. Spurgeon, "The Fullness of Christ—The Treasury of the Sacred Heart," *The Metropolitan Tabernacle Pulpit*, Vol. 10 (Passmore & Alabaster, 1864), 426–427.

2. Anne Lamott, *Traveling Mercies: Some Thoughts on Faith* (Pantheon Books, 1999).

4. Bind up the Injured

1. Brene Brown, *Atlas of The Heart: Mapping Meaningful Connection and the Language of Human Experience,* (Random House, 2021), 111
2. Brené Brown, *Atlas of The Heart: Mapping Meaningful Connection and the Language of Human Experience,* (Random House, 2021), 111-112.
3. Job 4:7-8; 11:6.
4. Job 8:3-6.
5. John 11:35.
6. Dale C. Bruner, *The Gospel of John: A Commentary* (Eerdmans, 2012), 678.
7. See Mark 1:40-42.
8. Romans 12:15, ESV.
9. 1 Corinthians 12:26.
10. Dr. Henry Cloud and Dr, John Townsend, *Boundaries: When to Say Yes How to Say No to Take Control of Your Life* (Zondervan, 1992), 33.
11. J.R.R. Tolkien, *The Return of the King,* (HarperCollinsPublishers, 2017), 1,230.
12. Kintsugi is a Japanese artform in which artists use gold to repair broken pottery, thereby making the pottery even more valuable and beautiful. This can serve as a reminder that the healed portions of our story are what give God (the potter) the glory.

5. Heal the Sick

1. *Imago Dei* means"image of God,"reminding us that every person carries God's likeness and inherent worth.
2. For a fuller exploration of this idea, along with practical tools for addressing underlying behaviors, check out Steve Carter's book *The Thing Beneath the Thing.*
3. Isaiah 53:3 (NLT).
4. Lecrae, unpublished remarks delivered at the Nazarene Youth Conference (NYC), Louisville, Kentucky, 2015.
5. 2 Corinthians 5:17, NLT.

6. Strengthen the Weak

1. Marcus Tullius Cicero, *On the Orator,* trans. E.W. Sutton and H. Rackham (Harvard University Press, 1942), III.221.
2. Matthew 6:23.
3. Eric J. Parks and Michele Cushatt, *FOLLOW: Learning the Way of Life with Jesus,* (Plum Creek Church, 2025), 245.
4. Matthew 5:16.
5. This language is borrowed from *The 100X Leader,* by Jeremie Kubiceck & Steve Cockram (John Wiley & Sons, Inc., 2019).
6. "The Nine" come from John Mark Comer's *Practicing the Way,* (WaterBrook, 2024), but the definitions are my own.
7. For a more in-depth exploration of spiritual practices, see John Mark Comer's, *Practicing the Way,* and Richard J. Foster's classic work, *Celebration of Discipline.*

7. Your Good Shepherd

1. N. T. Wright, *Simply Jesus: A New Vision of Who He Was, What He Did, and Why He Matters*, (HarperOne, 2011), 148.
2. Mark 2:17, NLT.

9. Simple Self-Care for Shepherds

1. Luke 22:44, ESV.
2. C.S. Lewis discusses this idea in *Letters to Malcolm: Chiefly on Prayer* (London: Geoffrey Bles, 1964), Letter 4.
3. The phrase, "Feelings are indicators, not dictators,"was popularized in Christian circles by Lysa TerKeurst in *Unglued: Making Wise Choices in the Midst of Raw Emotions* (Zondervan, 2012).
4. Hebrews 4:12, ESV.
5. Brennan Manning, quoted in DC Talk, "What If I Stumble?"on *Jesus Freak*, ForeFront Records, 1995.

ABOUT THE AUTHOR

Tomy A. Cummins is a pastor, communicator, and mental health advocate who serves as the Lead Student Pastor at Plum Creek Church in Castle Rock, Colorado. Across more than two decades of ministry, Tomy has helped create a student environment marked by psychological safety, biblical discipleship, and honest conversations about mental health. His work integrates the wisdom of scripture with evidence-based mental health practices, shaped through his training in Youth Mental Health First Aid (YMHFA), Teen Mental Health First Aid (TMHFA), LivingWorks safeTALK and ASIST, Soul Shop, and QPRT Suicide Risk Detection.

Tomy's passion is helping everyday followers of Jesus become healing, hopeful presences in the lives of those who are suffering by creating a rhythm of life that is deeply connected to the Creator. Whether teaching students, walking with families, training volunteers, or writing, his heart beats for the church to reflect the compassionate presence of the Good Shepherd.

Tomy lives in Castle Rock, Colorado, with his wife, Mendy, who is completing a dual-master's program in clinical mental health and school counseling at Denver Seminary, their two children, Laney Drew and Judah James, and an extremely affectionate golden doodle, Sir Chester Chauntavious Chewingston Esquire (Chewie for short). When he's not writing or preaching, Tomy enjoys time with his family, reading, playing disc golf, snowboarding, birdwatching, and cheering for the Oklahoma City Thunder like they can hear him from 600 miles away.